The

DIVINE EMBRACE

TYNDALE HOUSE PUBLISHERS, INC.
WHEATON, ILLINOIS

Library of Congress Cataloging-in-Publication Data

Gire, Ken.
  The divine embrace / Ken Gire.
    p. cm.
Includes bibliographical references.
  ISBN 0-8423-7023-4 (hc) ISBN 0-8423-7071-4 (sc)
  1. Christian life. 2. Dance—Religious aspects—Christianity. I. Title.
  BV4501.3.G565 2003
  248.4—dc21   2003005224

For my brother, Roger,

About whom I could say a lot of wonderful things,

All of which would probably embarrass him

If I put them in print.

Except this:

He loves Jesus.

I am proud to be his brother.

Privileged to be his friend.

For Ken Gire's speaking schedule,
booking information, and additional resources,
see the ministry's Web site at
www. reflectiveliving.com

CONTENTS

THE AUTHOR'S PRAYER

Dear Jesus,
I ask one thing for the readers of this book,
that they love you more when they finally put it down
than they did when they first picked it up.
Amen.

*If we are indifferent to the art of dancing,
we have failed to understand, not merely the
supreme manifestation of physical life, but also
the supreme symbol of spiritual life.*

HAVELOCK ELLIS, *THE DANCE OF LIFE*

THE DANCE

I hope you never fear those mountains in the distance,
Never settle for the path of least resistance . . .
Give the heavens above more than just a passing glance,
And when you get the choice to sit it out or dance,
I hope you dance. . . . I hope you dance.

LEE ANN WOMACK, "I HOPE YOU DANCE"

T he first time I thought of my relationship with
Christ as a divine embrace that resembled a dance
was at a thrift store.

I sometimes browse the book section of the Good-
will store in downtown Colorado Springs, hoping for
an occasional treasure but settling most often for simply
a good deal. Before I leave, I always check the shelf that
holds the fifty-cent cassettes in hopes of finding good
company for my thirty-minute trip home.

One day I might take home the Pointer Sisters.

Another day Pavarotti.

This day it was a collection of classical music that
made the ride.

The first selection on the tape was the "Emperor
Waltz" by Johann Strauss II. It began with a simple
musical phrase that seemed easy enough to dance to. In
my mind's eye, my feet followed the notes effortlessly.

Then the music swelled into a theme so noble I felt
my back arching and my shoulders squaring in
response. Something about that moment touched me,

and my eyes glistened with the beginning of tears. I felt in the presence of royalty . . . and ennobled by that presence. At that moment, I became committed to the dance, committed to following the music wherever it would lead.

When the easy, light-footed rhythms returned, I felt lifted by them. Quite unexpectedly, though, the music took a confusing turn. It seemed unsure of itself, as if it had lost its way on the page. I didn't like it. I didn't like the dissonance. Or the stumbling sense of uncertainty it brought to the dance.

Before I could break the embrace, however, the waltz returned to its familiar themes. I found myself once again being swept away by the music. It was exhilarating.

Toward the end of the waltz, the music slowed, so much so that it felt as if it were going to stop completely. Just before it did, a flute came in, and one protracted note from that flute ushered me to a crescendo so stirring it brought tears once again to my eyes.

I played the waltz again—and again tears brimmed my eyes—both at the beginning, where the noble strain of music swells, and at the end, where the music crests.

I wondered why. There were no lyrics, no words to stir my imagination. There was only the music.

As I pondered my reactions to the "Emperor Waltz," the story of Jesus and his disciples came to mind. I reflected on the beginning notes of the waltz, and it seemed to capture how the disciples must have felt when Christ first invited them to follow him and become fishers of men. How easy those initial steps must have been. Walking with Jesus from town to town, leisurely asking him questions along the way. Witnessing the miracle he performed at the wedding in Cana, tapping their toes to the festive music. Watching him interact with people, loving them, teaching them, consoling them.

Then I thought about the next section in the dance, where the music swells. I thought of my response to it, and it seemed similar to how the disciples must have reacted when they first realized who Jesus was. It happens to all of us at one time or another in our relationship with Christ. Some miraculous moment opens our eyes, the way it did with the disciples, and we ask ourselves, as they asked themselves, "'Who is this? Even the wind and the waves obey him!'" (Mark 4:41, NIV).

At that moment, we realize for the first time the extraordinary dignity that has been conferred on us, that the Emperor himself has called our name, extended his hand, and invited us not only to be with him but to partner with him in the work he is doing in the world.

The dissonant part of the dance confused me. If I'd had the choice, I would have edited it out. But it was not my dance and therefore not my prerogative. My life has gone through three such movements—confusing times, each of which I would have edited out, too, if I'd had the choice. I'm sure the disciples would have wanted to do the same with some of the disorienting places to which they were led.

I reflected on the end of the waltz, where the music slows and it seems as if life itself is slowing. *Maybe this is how it all ends,* I thought. One by one the notes of life drop off, dwindle to stillness, then silence. Instead of silence, however, a hopeful note sounds. It is the note that ushers us into the ballroom of heaven. It is a moment so stunningly resplendent that it takes my breath away.

It may be hard to imagine . . . but try.

Imagine yourself in a ballroom. Imagine that the Emperor, the Lord Jesus himself, has tapped your shoulder. Hear his voice as he speaks your name and asks you to dance. It is not a dance you have done before. You're uncertain about it, maybe a little fearful—hesitant to participate. But take a chance; step out onto the dance floor. As the Emperor draws you near, look into his eyes. Place your palm in his. And follow his lead.

Listen to the "Emperor Waltz" and allow yourself to be swept away.

When the waltz is over, pause to catch your breath; then relive the experience.

What were you feeling during the dance? Excited that you were on the dance floor? Honored that Jesus picked you to be his partner? Ennobled by the dignity of the dance? Confused at places? Uncertain of your next step? Out of breath at the pace? A little dizzy? Afraid you might trip and fall? Embarrassed that you stepped on his toes? Exhilarated when it was over?

All of those feelings you will experience in the course of following Christ. It's natural to feel uncertain about a dance you have never done before. It's natural to be fearful, even hesitant.

Dance lessons would help, wouldn't they?

But maybe it's not so much lessons in dancing we need as lessons in loving, because the Christian life is about intimacy, not technique. The Lord of the dance doesn't want us worrying about our feet. He doesn't want us wondering about the steps ahead. He merely wants us to feel the music, fall into his arms, and follow his lead.

There are places he wants to take us on the dance floor, things he wants to show us, feelings he wants to share with us, words he wants to whisper in our ear. This is what the divine embrace is—an invitation to a more intimate relationship with Christ, one exhilarating, ennobling, uncertain step at a time.

7

We have a choice, you and I. And it's a choice we make every day, throughout the day. The choice is this:

We can dance.

Or we can sit it out.

If we dance, we may step on his toes. And he may step on ours. We may stumble and bump into other people. We may fall on our faces and make fools of ourselves. People may talk, they may avoid us, they may even ridicule us.

If you fear those things, you may want to sit it out.

If you do, you won't have to worry. You'll be safe in your seat along the wall.

You'll also miss the dance.

More importantly, you'll miss the romance.

At some time or another, I have chosen to sit it out. Fear was a big reason. Fear of the attention it would bring—and perhaps the criticism. Fear of embarrass-ment and possible estrangement. Fear of not being in control of my life, my career, my future. Fear of being led to places that would be uncomfortable, even painful.

There are two things I have learned from the divine embrace.

That perfect love really does cast out fear.

And that I would rather dance poorly with Jesus than sit perfectly with anyone else.

THE PRELUDE
TO THE DANCE

*It was later on while we were eating that Dr. MacNeill
made his way across the room to me. . . .
The music snaked across the floor, swirled around
my ankles, set my toes to tapping. Dr. MacNeill saw.
"Come on, Christy. Into the circle we go."
. . . I was spun through the air, blood racing with the
music, aware of the Doctor's face close to mine, sometimes
half-smiling, sometimes laughing, drawing me to him.*

CATHERINE MARSHALL, *CHRISTY*

F riedrich Nietzsche, the German philosopher who popularized the "God is dead" movement, once wrote in a letter to a friend: "If these Christians want me to believe in their god, they'll have to sing better songs, they'll have to look more like people who have been saved, they'll have to wear on their countenance the joy of the beatitudes. I could only believe in a god who dances."

What Nietzsche failed to realize is that our God, who is very much alive, *is* a God who dances. What we Christians sometimes fail to realize is that he is a God who dances *with us*.

To speak of our relationship with Christ as a dance is, of course, to speak metaphorically. But it is also to speak biblically. In the parable of the Prodigal Son, for example, the father's joy at his son's return was cause for a celebration—at which, the text says, there was feasting, music, and *dancing*. In Matthew 11:17, Jesus also uses the metaphor to describe the generation that rejected him. "We played the flute for you," he told them, "and you did not dance." Jesus invited them to dance, longed for them to dance, and was heartbroken when they didn't.

The image of the dance is a picture of two people in love, partnered in joyful embrace, moving in step to the tune of beautiful music. The image of dancing with Jesus is awkward for some, especially for men. Men are accustomed to thinking of their relationship with Christ in terms of masculine images, such as soldiers, athletes, farmers, or builders. Dancing, especially with Jesus as our partner, is a particularly difficult image for men to embrace, because it is from a feminine set of images. Yet there are a number of decidedly feminine images the Bible uses to describe our relationship with Christ. The image, for example, that compares our relationship with Christ to that of a bride and groom (see John 3:29; Ephesians 5:22-23). In the upper room, Jesus told his disciples that he was leaving to prepare a place for them so he could receive them to himself and be with them forever (see John 14:2-3). The image is that of a bridegroom preparing for the honeymoon and a life of happily-ever-aftering. In the final pages of the Scriptures, Christ's undying love for his bride culminates in the celebration of his union with her (see Revelation 19:7).

When the Bible talks about our work for Christ, images from the battlefield or the athletic arena are fitting comparisons. But when it talks about the love that Christ has for us, it is such a passionate love that the only imagery that comes close to capturing the feeling is a romantic one.

The Song of Solomon, for example, is full of such imagery. Though primarily a song about the all-consuming love of a king for his bride, on a secondary level it illustrates Christ's passion for his bride and his patient yet persistent pursuit of her. When men think in terms of a romantic relationship, they usually see themselves as the pursuer, not the one being pursued. But throughout the course of human history, God has been the pursuer. His love is an initiating love. Our role is to respond. We love, John tells us, because God first loved us (see 1 John 4:19). We pursue him because, and only because, he first pursued us.

I see an illustration of that pursuit in the movie *Patch Adams,* starring Robin Williams and Monica Potter. The film is based on the life of Hunter "Patch" Adams, a real-life physician known for his handlebar mustache, outlandishly colorful and mismatched clothes, and his antiestablishment philosophy of treating patients. When Adams entered medical school, he was determined to practice medicine differently, to treat the whole patient and not simply the patient's disease. Humor, he felt, was a big part of the treatment.

For me, the most compelling scenes in the movie are those that chronicle the progression of Patch's relationship with Carin. From the first day that Patch sees her in one of his classes, he is smitten. After class he approaches her, but she rudely rejects his advances.

The next time they meet is in a small study group in the library. The group is meeting to go over questions for an upcoming exam, but Patch broaches the subject of caring for patients as people rather than merely treating their diseases. Frustrated, Carin walks out. Catching up with her, Patch tries to connect with her, but again she walks away, thinking he is simply a nonconformist who will sooner or later flunk out.

Her attitude changes, however, a few days later when she reads the posted test scores. After finding her score, a 79, she looks to the top of the page and discovers that Patch has the second highest grade in the class: a 98. That proves to be a turning point in their relationship.

Now seeing him as intellectually superior, she begins to take him seriously—spending time with him, listening to his theories on patient care, and laughing at his jokes.

In a later scene, Patch throws a birthday party for Carin by filling a room with balloons and friends. In the midst of the ensuing chaos, he reads her a love poem. After the party, he walks her to her dorm. Carin is deeply moved by how nice he has been to her, and she tells him that nobody had ever done anything like that for her before.

More and more, Carin is drawn into the relationship and into Patch's work. Along with a number of other volunteers, she helps Patch renovate a dilapidated old house that symbolizes a new paradigm in doctor-patient relationships.

Later that night, in a vulnerable moment on the porch steps, Patch leans toward Carin to kiss her. Instead of responding to this gesture of affection, she turns her head.

"What are we?" Patch asks, trying to understand why she continues to shun his affection.

"All of my life," she says, as tears brim her eyes, "men have been attracted to me." She turns to look at Patch as a tear breaks its banks and spills down her cheek. "*All* my life."

At that moment we understand that Carin has been sexually abused over the course of her life, from child-hood into adulthood.

"I hated men *so* much," she says. "And then I met *you.*"

Suddenly everything is clear. We understand why Carin pushes men away and why for so long she has pushed Patch away. Instead of getting his feelings hurt and reacting or getting weary of the rejection and walk-ing away, Patch pursued her all the more. He engaged her in conversation, humoring her. He invited her on a late-night visit to help some patients, threw a party for her, shared his hopes and his dreams with her, never giving up on her, never writing her off, never leaving or forsaking her.

When I see how patiently yet persistently Patch pursues Carin, I think of Jesus.

Thinking of him, I think of some of the women he met—the woman at the well, the woman caught in adultery, the prostitute who wept at his feet— and I can't help but feel compassion for the hurt little girl in them all. I think of their encounters with men over the course of their lives, and when I think of their encounters with Jesus, Carin's words come to mind.

15

"I hated men *so* much . . . and then I met *you.*"

Does anyone know how many men have been attracted to these women, and for how long? Does anyone know what those men did to them, what they took from them, what they left behind? Does anyone know the seamy memories they lived with? or the sweaty nightmares they woke from?

Jesus knows. He also knows the hurt *we* have experienced along the way to growing up and the defense mechanisms we have erected to protect ourselves from being hurt again. Still he pursues us, longing to gather us in his arms and enfold us into a romantic and adventurous future with him.

That pursuit is the prelude to the dance.

When I think back on the way Jesus has pursued me over the years, the way he pursues me still, I love him more at the end of those thoughts than I did at the beginning.

Suddenly, I understand the prostitute's tears. Not only why she wept them. But why she wept them where she did.

On Jesus' feet.

The feet that had pursued her.

The same feet that pursue each one of us, so patiently yet persistently.

In spite of all the paintings and icons, it is hard for me to visualize what Jesus looked like. What has been helpful to me has not been imagining his face, but rather his feet. I sometimes imagine myself washing them. Taking a soft Mediterranean sponge and dipping it into a basin of warm water, then rubbing the day's dust off the Savior's feet. And feeling so privileged to be doing so.

Sometimes I imagine just holding one of those feet in my hands, and pressing it to my face. Feeling his heartbeat in it, warming it . . . warming me.

I don't need to say anything to him.

He doesn't need to say anything to me.

It is enough that he is near.

And that I am at his feet.

THE INTIMACY
OF THE DANCE

I danced for the scribe
And the pharisee,
But they would not dance
And they wouldn't follow me.
I danced for the fishermen,
For James and John—
They came with me
And the dance went on.

Dance, then, wherever you may be,
I am the Lord of the Dance, said he,
And I'll lead you all, wherever you may be,
And I'll lead you all in the Dance, said he.

SYDNEY CARTER, "LORD OF THE DANCE"

The first time I visited Israel was as a speaker for a tour group. One of the places I was scheduled to speak was the Mount of the Beatitudes, which slopes gently into the Sea of Galilee. The Church of the Beatitudes is there, which is where I thought I was going to speak. Behind a pulpit of some sort, I supposed, where I could spread out my notes and lay open my Bible. And with a microphone, I assumed, which I need because my voice doesn't project well.

Speaking used to terrify me. So the pulpit was necessary not so much to hold my notes as to hide me. And I needed the microphone because whenever I had to project my voice, I became even more self-conscious. Which is why I needed the notes, because when I got nervous, I would forget things. Which is why I needed the pulpit, so in case I forgot something, I could glance at my notes.

After dinner I was told I would not be speaking in the church. Instead, I would be speaking on the same hillside where Jesus had spoken. "Isn't that going be a wonderful experience?" the tour director said.

Open air. No microphone. And no pulpit.
Which meant no notes.
Wonderful.

I stayed up all night trying to put the words I had
crafted into my head, hoping they would stay there
until it was time for me to speak. Around four in the
morning I finished. Too late to go to bed. Too early to
go to breakfast. So I went outside and sat on the shoreline, praying in the dark that all the words would somehow come out right and might be used in some way in
the lives of those who were coming to hear them.

Within an hour, the darkness faded to halftones,
revealing spectral images of a flat lake and a featureless
landscape on the far shore. A hint of pink on the clouds
came next. And with it, a shiver of pink on the water.
The gray sky softened to blue. The blushing clouds to
yellow. With color came dimension. Shadows sought
refuge in caves and ravines, deepening the landscape
and giving the muted greens and browns the courage
to show themselves. As the sun rose, it seemed that the
sky, the clouds, the hills, the lake, and their retinue of
attendants had assembled at this royal court for some
long-awaited moment of coronation.

I sat for a long time, watching the regal procession.
I watched as the satin surface of the lake caught a
breeze and rippled its smooth folds toward shore. I
watched kitelike birds hover over the water, waiting for
a glint of sun off the scales of shallow-swimming fish.
I watched the town rub the sleep from its eyes, yawn-
ing itself awake, stretching, then slapping its bare feet
to the cool ground of another day.

22

And as I watched, it came to me: *It all started here. Here,* in *this* place, the world that had sat in darkness saw a great light. With the dawning of that light came color. Dimension. The first stirrings of life.

It was *here,* on *these* shores, that Jesus first said to Peter and Andrew as they were hunched over their nets: "Follow Me, and I will make you fishers of men" (Matthew 4:9).

It was here that he said to James and John as they were mooring their boats: "Follow me."

On this same shoreline, the Lord of the dance had picked his first partners. "Follow me, and I will lead you all in the dance," said he.

23

But where was he leading? And what, besides their nets and boats, would they have to leave behind? How long of a dance would this be? How difficult were the steps? And how dizzying the turns?

A lot of unknowns, not just for them but for us.

Jesus comes to us, noted Albert Schweitzer, much the way he came to the first disciples: "He comes to us as One Unknown, without a name, as of old, by the lakeside, He came to those who knew Him not. He speaks to us the same word: 'Follow thou me!' and sets us to the tasks which He has to fulfill for our time. He commands. And to those who obey Him, whether they be wise or simple, He will reveal Himself in the toils, the conflicts, the sufferings which they shall pass through in His fellowship, and, as an ineffable mystery, they shall learn in their own experience Who He is."

The men who followed Jesus were never the same. Neither was the world. And *here* is where it all started.

On *this* lakeside. No other moment in the Holy Land compared to that one on the shores of Galilee as I watched the ascending sun bestow life and warmth and color on everything it touched.

I felt honored to be seeing the same sun that dawned on those fishermen, on those shores, so many sunrises ago. I also felt humbled. Humbled for the dawn that so many sunrises ago had come to my shores, giving life and depth and color to everything it touched. Humbled, too, by the invitation to follow him.

Before Jesus called the disciples to ministry, he called them to intimacy. Following came first, fishing came later. Before he called them to represent him, he called them to *be* with him. Jesus appointed the twelve that they might be *with* him and that he might send them out to preach and to have authority over demons (see Mark 3:14-15). Before he sent them out, he drew them close. He went out with them publicly so they could hear him teach and see him heal the sick and cast out demons (see Luke 6:12-19). At times, he withdrew with them privately so they could be with him without distraction (see Luke 9:10). Even as he was leaving the earth, he promised he would always be *with* them (see Matthew 28:20). And later, Luke tells us, the credential by which the disciples were recognized was that of "having been with Jesus" (Acts 4:13).

24

Of the twelve he chose to be with him more closely, three were closest: Peter, James, and John. He took only those three into the room when he raised Jairus's daughter from the dead (see Luke 8:51). He took only those three onto the Mount of Transfiguration, where they were given a glimpse of the glory that awaited him (see Mark 9:2). He took only those three into the garden of Gethsemane, where they were given a glimpse of the agony that also awaited him (see Mark 14:32-33).

Of those three disciples, John had the most intimate relationship with Jesus. In John's Gospel, he describes himself as the disciple "whom Jesus loved." It was John who was nearest to Jesus at the Last Supper, resting his head on Jesus' chest (John 13:23). And when Jesus announced that one of the disciples would betray him, Peter gestured to John and asked him to ask who it would be. Then leaning back on Christ's chest, John said, "Lord, who is it?" (John 13:25).

25

John was the only disciple mentioned at the Cross (see John 19:26-27). He was the first disciple at Christ's tomb (see John 20:3-5). And the first to recognize his voice when Jesus called to them from the shore (see John 21:7). Jesus entrusted John not only with great responsibility—the care of his mother, Mary (see John 19:26-27)—but also with great revelation (see Revelation 1:1).

If I could be anyone in times past—any king, any warrior, any prophet, any person of power or position, *anyone*—I would want to be John. I would want to go where he went, see what he saw, and hear what he heard.

When John rested his head against the Savior's chest, he didn't feel the least bit awkward about it or the least bit inappropriate. Imagine what that must have been like. Feeling the warmth of the Savior's chest against your face. Hearing the beating of his heart in your ear.

Imagine what it must have been like at the cross. Seeing every indignity done to Christ, and the dignity in every one of his responses. Hearing every gasp for air, every offer of grace.

Imagine the honor of being entrusted with the care of Mary. With that one gift, John was given access to every childhood memory she had of Jesus, every story, every thought she had ever pondered in her heart, every startling joy, every stabbing pain.

And if that were not enough, Jesus gave John still another gift, visiting him in his loneliness on the island of Patmos and revealing not just himself in his glory but the glory of the world to come.

Imagine what it would be like to love Jesus the way John loved him. That would be more than any of us could ever want, more than we could ever hope for, more than we could ever dream of.

And yet, as hard as it is to imagine, *more* is what we are offered.

Even more.

———————

26   Having grown up in the heat and humidity of north central Texas and now living in the cool mountain air of central Colorado, I sometimes feel like Dorothy in *The Wizard of Oz,* who was plucked by a tornado from the black-and-white Kansas prairie and plopped into an enchanted land, alive with color. I have loved every day of my ten years in Colorado.

I have seen wonderful things here. A breath of winter fog transforming common trees into the magical forests of Narnia. Lightning so dramatic it seemed mythological in its fury.

I have heard wonderful things, too, such as a wake of migrating geese, honking low overhead. Rain so gentle it seemed the kindness of God, coming near.

Much of this I have experienced while driving toward the Front Range of the Rocky Mountains on the way to my office. Sculpted by the hand of Almighty God, the mountains reveal something of who he is, something of the wisdom of his ways, what he values, how much he loves us.

27

It is sacred ground I travel. Sometimes I forget *how* sacred.

And then one day the clouds part, and a pail of sun splashes the dark flanks of the mountain. At once, everything shimmers, and I see it all as if for the first time. Fields of tawny grass slow-dancing to the music of a far-off wind. Above them, white splotches of aspen, their shivering leaves reaching for the warmth of a sudden sun. Farther up, an army of Ponderosa pine marches in broken ranks up the foothills, toward a stalwart row standing sentry along the ridge. How long have these good soldiers stood, so tall, so straight, and so vigilant in their assigned duty?

All of nature stands in allegiance to God. Bowing before him the way the grass bows before the wind. Reaching out to him the way the aspen do, depending on the warmth of his sun for their life. Standing stead-fast like the pines, every regiment within the natural order taking its appointed place, accomplishing its assigned task.

When I think of these things, I'm reminded it is not common ground I travel every day on my way to work. How common of me to have thought so.

Every day I travel other ground that is also sacred. I'm referring to the Scriptures, whose grandeur has become so familiar that I sometimes take it for granted. Until a spill of morning sun washes over a familiar passage, and suddenly I have new eyes, as if seeing it for the first time.

I'm thinking of the familiar passage in John 13–17 known as the Upper Room Discourse. To put Christ's words in their proper emotional context, we need to know only one thing: In less than twenty-four hours, he would be dead. He knew that. So this was a time of last things. It was not only his last supper, it was his last time with the disciples before he died. It was a time of last looks, last embraces, last words.

At the end of the evening, Jesus prays a last prayer for them. He prays not only on behalf of his disciples but for everyone who would believe in him through their words. In the last words of that prayer, Jesus, speaking to his Father, asks "that the love you have for me may be in them" (John 17:26, NIV).

Do you hear what he is asking?

Can you feel the breathtaking grandeur in his petition?

When I first realized what Jesus was requesting, it stopped me in my tracks. It stopped me the way a full double rainbow stops me whenever I see one, with its arching wonder so startling, its rain-washed colors so vivid, its promise so hopeful, extending not just to Noah and his family but to each and every generation that followed. So it is with this prayer. It is not just for that first privileged gathering of disciples. It is for each and every disciple that has followed after them.

Which means it's for me.

And for you.

We're told in the Scriptures that Jesus now sits at the right hand God, where he intercedes for us. He *lives* to make intercession for us, according to the author of Hebrews. We are in his heart. Which means we are also in his prayers. Our name is on his lips. What do you think Jesus asks when he brings our name before his Father? Our daily bread? Surely. Our need for forgiveness? That, too. Our prayers for those we love? Certainly. But there is something more, something greater, that is the deepest longing of his heart.

29

When my name is on the Savior's lips, I believe he is asking that the love the Father has for him would also be in me.

Is it possible? Is it even remotely possible that I could love Jesus that way? It seems a yellow-brick-road flight of the imagination, as far away from reality as skipping off to the Emerald City; as far-fetched a fantasy as a wizard who grants brains to scarecrows, hearts to tin men, and courage to cowardly lions. It is too incredible to believe. How could you and I, living here on earth, possibly love Jesus the way his Father in heaven loves him?

Love him the way the crowds loved him—those

who flocked to hear him preach, who stood on tiptoe to
see him perform miracles?

Possibly.

Love him the way the brokenhearted loved him—
the diseased, the demon-possessed, the down-and-out
whose lives he forever changed?

I hope so, but honestly I don't think so.

Love him the way the disciples loved him, who left
everything to follow him?

Doubtful.

Love him the way John loved him, the one who was
closest to him, who leaned against his chest at that last
supper, who followed him to the cross?

Even more doubtful.

But love him the way his own Father loves him?

Impossible. Simply and utterly impossible.

Yet if it were not possible, why would Jesus pray
such a prayer?

Why would he put such a hope in our hearts if that
hope could never be fulfilled?

It comes down to this. Either Jesus, like the Wizard
of Oz, is "a very good man but . . . a very bad wizard."
Or else he is the Son of God. The *only* Son of God. The
dearly beloved Son of God. If he is, who could possibly
please the Father more? And what prayer could possibly
delight the Father more in answering? The logic seems
inescapable. Wonderfully, marvelously, deliriously inescapable.

Ever since that sun-drenched moment of grace
when the clouds over that verse parted, the focus of
my life has changed. Now so many mornings when

I awake, with my head still on the pillow and sleep still in my eyes, I thank God for the gift of a new day. I ask that I not take for granted the generosity of another day, that I might be attentive to the gifts he wants me to receive and also to the ones he wants me to give. Then I ask that by evening I would love Jesus more than I did that morning. I know that I will love him more if I see him more and hear him more, so I ask to see even the slightest glimpse of him during the day and hear even the smallest echo of his voice above the other voices in my day.

Because Jesus promised to disclose himself inti-mately to us, I have every confidence that in some way or another he will make good on that promise. The anticipation heightens my awareness to the ordinary moments of my day. Remarkable things happen when I pay attention. Here and there I actually do see some-thing of his presence. Now and then I really do hear something of his voice.

31

In every act of kindness, I see something of Jesus. In every act of courage, I see him, too. I see it in the courage of William Wallace when I watch the movie *Braveheart.* I see it in the kindness of how Jesus pursued Anne Lamott after her abortion, which I read about in her spiritual memoir, *Traveling Mercies.*

Now when I go to bed at night, with my head resting on the pillow, my eyes closed, I thank God for the day, sifting through what I have found there. I reflect on the many gifts that were extended to me and the various hands through which those gifts came. I thank him for those gifts, especially those that had something of Jesus in them. When I can isolate and identify those gifts, I realize that I love Jesus more at that moment before sleep than I had when I awoke that morning.

These are the mornings and evenings of my life. And this is how I want to live for the rest of my life—loving Jesus more today than I did yesterday, and more tomorrow than I do today. I want to live that way, every day, until the last day of my life, when I awake in his arms.

I know it sounds like a ruby-slippers kind of prayer.

But after two years of praying this way, it has taken me to some wonderful places.

It has taken me to a more beautiful place in my relationship with Jesus. I do love him more. And loving him more, I have found that I love all that he loves more. I love his Father more. I love his Spirit more. I love his Word more. I love the world for which he died more. I love heaven more, because that is where *he* is, preparing a place for us.

A place he called Paradise.

As incredible as it seems, there *is* a place over the rainbow where troubles melt like lemon drops, where the dreams that you dare to dream really do come true.

But until the day when we go to that place or the day when Jesus returns to take us there, we must live our lives *under* the rainbow . . . where the road ahead is not paved with yellow bricks. Sometimes it has no bricks at all, only the sharp-edged remains of our shattered dreams.

What we find under the rainbow is not an easier

road to travel but traveling mercies *for* the road, however long or hard it may be.

One of those mercies is that along the way we are given glimpses of the one we now love only from afar.

Something happens to us in those moments. A shift in focus. We find that our eyes are no longer on the steepness of the road or the sharpness of the rocks beneath our feet but on him who has gone before us. When we see Jesus, however briefly, however indistinctly, our hearts begin to ache. In that moment and because of that moment, we love him more. And if we don't love him more, at least we long to.

33

It is in those moments that we discover where the Lord of the Dance has been leading us all along—into a deeper love for him. A deeper love than the disciples had for him. A deeper love than even John had.

Jesus leads us in a dance that moves around his Father's heart, in ever tighter circles, until at last we are so close to the love that is at the center of the universe that we feel it, every throbbing beat of it.

And when that happens, the beating of his heart and the beating of ours become one.

THE STILL POINT
OF THE DANCE

Except for the point, the still point,
There would be no dance,
And there is only the dance.

T. S. ELIOT, *FOUR QUARTETS*

I n the Japanese film *Shall We Dance?* a female dance
instructor walks away from a male student and
blurts out in exasperation, "It takes men three times
longer to learn."

Most men do take longer. Some never learn. And
some don't learn until later in life. Socrates, for example, was seventy before he learned to dance. What
motivated him was the awareness that all his life he
had neglected an essential part of himself.

Sometimes it takes that same awareness to get us
to dance with Jesus: a growing sense of having
neglected something essential. That was what was
being neglected in the home of Mary and Martha the
day Jesus showed up. Seeing him filling the doorway
sent Martha into a scurry of activity. A meal needed
to be prepared. Promptly. And perfectly. After all, it
was for Jesus.

Somewhere in the kitchen, though, she lost sight of
whom the meal was for. Maybe it wasn't for Jesus, not
ultimately anyway. Maybe it wasn't so much about his

need to have a meal as much as it was her need to prepare one.

Martha was the dutiful sister. She had that in common with the dutiful, older brother in the parable of the Prodigal Son. If you recall, the dutiful brother was also the critical one. He was serving in the fields when his younger brother came home, and when he approached the house, "he heard music and dancing" (Luke 15:25). He drew near, but not to join in the dancing. He drew near to debate. The debate centered around how dutiful he had been, in contrast to his wasteful younger brother.

Duty destroys relationships, because duty reduces relationships to a to-do list. The firstborn son looked at his service to his father as a checklist of commandments. My own children don't work for me, but if they did, I wouldn't want them serving me because it was their job. I would want them serving me because it was their joy.

Duty also destroys joy. Whatever joy we may derive from our duties is related to a performance, not a person. If our performance is the source of our joy, it will also be the source of our pride, which in the end will undo us. That seems to be the case with the dutiful brother serving in the fields as well as the dutiful sister serving in the kitchen.

Perhaps that is also what drives so much of our own activity.

The point isn't that activity and intimacy are mutually exclusive. The point is that our activity *for* Christ should grow out of our intimacy *with* him. If we are

near him, continually beholding him, he will tell us
what he wants from the kitchen and when he wants it.

That, I believe, is the most efficient way to serve
him.

It is also the most exhilarating.

Martha is a picture of the frenetic church—
distracted by all its preparations, worried and bothered
about so many things. Mary is a picture of the focused
church—seated at Christ's feet, gazing into his eyes,
and listening to his words.

Jesus' feelings about Mary's devotion are captured
in a scene from Goethe's novel *The Sorrows of Young
Werther,* in which the main character is captivated by
a woman he sees on the dance floor. "You should see
her dance! She concentrates so completely—heart
and soul—on the dance itself; her whole body is in
harmony, as carefree and as ingenuous as if nothing
else mattered, as if she had no other thoughts or feelings; and I am certain that at those moments everything else vanishes from her sight."

That is how I want to dance with Jesus. That is the
kind of focus I want. As if nothing else mattered. As if
everything else vanished from sight. For I would rather
see his face and have everything else blur in my peripheral vision than to have every peripheral thing in focus
and miss seeing him.

THE STILL POINT

In his book titled *Reaching Out,* Henri Nouwen
describes the "still point" of the dance, not only what
happens there but also how it happens. "Being useless

and silent in the presence of our God belongs to the core of all prayer. In the beginning we often hear our own unruly inner noises more loudly than God's voice. This is at times very hard to tolerate. But slowly, very slowly, we discover that the silent time makes us quiet and deepens our awareness of ourselves and God. Then, very soon, we start missing these moments when we are deprived of them, and before we are fully aware of it an inner momentum has developed that draws us more and more into silence and closer to that still point where God speaks to us."

The still point of the dance is the adoring gaze. It is the look of someone falling in love.

The still point of the dance of life is illustrated in a scene from the 1998 movie version of *Les Misérables*. Throughout the film, which is set in nineteenth century France, we see law and grace take on flesh and blood in the characters of Javert and Valjean. Javert is a police officer whose life is a tireless and ultimately tragic pursuit of trying to fulfill every jot and tittle of the law. Valjean's life, in contrast, is a gradual and beautiful outworking of the kindness of God, which he shared so freely with those whose lives were in such desperate need of it.

40 Valjean is mayor of the town of Montreuil-sur-Mer, where he owns a factory. One of his factory employees is a poor woman named Fantine, who is struggling to support her young daughter living in another town. When it is discovered that Fantine has an illegitimate child, the other women working in the factory complain to the foreman, who dismisses her. Destitute,

Fantine sells everything she can in order to continue supporting her daughter. She sells her locket, her hair, but finally runs out of things to sell. And so she takes to the streets, selling the one thing she has left. Herself.

One cold winter night, she is standing on a lamplit corner with other streetwalkers plying their trade. As she offers herself to a group of passing men, they surround her and mock her, shoving snow in her mouth and forcing it down her dress. They push her, grope her, and knock her to the cold, hard ground.

Standing in the shadows and watching all this is Javert. Stepping into the light, he breaks up the disturbance. As Fantine struggles to her feet, he slaps her in the face. Blood seeps from the corner of her mouth. He dismisses the men but arrests her. Holding a hurried court at the jail, Javert takes a quilled pen and records her punishment.

"Six months in prison," he decrees.

"What about Cosette?" she pleads. "What about *her?* If I don't send money—"

Javert is unsympathetic. Sin has its consequences, and she has sinned, so she must pay those consequences. That is the law.

Fantine begs him to hear her side of the story. In tears she acknowledges her sin, promising not to do it again.

But Javert, like the law, is stern and indifferent. "You're still getting six months."

The mayor enters the room. Having heard an eyewitness account and now seeing the way the woman has been humiliated, he frees her.

"You don't have the authority to do away with justice," replies Javert, his face set with indignation.

"I *do* have the authority. I can order her to be released. The decision is mine. She's free."

"She will not go free as long as I am in charge of this post."

The mayor dismisses Javert. "I *am* the final judicial authority here, and *I* say she is innocent."

Javert stiffens. "You are the mayor, the personification of order, morality, government, in fact. You don't have the right to forgive her."

Ignoring the preachment, Valjean turns to Fantine. "You're free to go."

Hearing the news, she faints.

In the next scene, the mayor has carried the weakened woman to his home, where a doctor has just examined her. The doctor isn't sure she will live through the night and asks if there is someone who could watch over her. Valjean volunteers. Bringing a bowl of water and setting it on the nightstand, he takes a washcloth, dips it in the water, gently touching her face with its coolness and its cleanness.

"I don't know why you're being so kind," she says, speaking through her bloodied mouth and looking up at him with her sunken eyes.

"You need to rest," he says.

In return for his kindness, she offers the one thing she has to give: her body.

But sex is not his motive. Nor will he accept it as his reward.

"Don't worry. I'm going to bring your daughter

here. I'll send the money to bring Cosette here. She'll attend a school and you won't have any worries."

Trembling, she says. "But you don't understand. I'm a *whore*. And Cosette has no father."

The way Fantine says the word *whore* and the look on her face as she says it, you feel the disdain she feels for herself, the utter disgust.

"She has the Lord," Valjean assures her. "He is her father. And you are his creation. In his eyes, you've never been anything but an innocent, beautiful person."

The moment is as incandescent as anything Rembrandt ever painted. It is framed by music that delicately focuses our attention to the grace of the moment.

The combination of strength and gentleness in Valjean reminds me of the encounter between Jesus and the woman caught in adultery (see John 8). The teachers of the law, accompanied by the Pharisees, are the ones who caught her and brought her to Jesus, throwing her into the middle of the crowd, where she stood disheveled and trembling, her fate once again at the hands of men.

Can you imagine how that woman felt when Jesus stood up for her, saved her from the stones, and set her free?

"Woman, . . . did no one condemn you?"

"No one, Lord."

"Neither do I condemn you. Go . . . and sin no more."

I saw something of Jesus in that moment in *Les Misérables*. And my heart ached—I mean *ached*. It was so easy to see why sinners flocked to Jesus, why they fell at his feet, wept at his feet, and washed them with their tears. What it must have been like to be in his presence. In his eyes and in his words was a grace that passed human understanding. His voice so calmly reassuring. His hands so protective as they cupped themselves around the dimly burning wicks he encountered. His touch so tender as it straightened the bruised reeds he met along the way.

"But you don't understand. I'm a *whore*."

"No, it is *you* who doesn't understand," Jesus seems to be saying. "Because if you knew, if *only* you knew, your heart would burst trying to hold all the love the Lord has for you, all the tender feelings, all the affection. Do you know how precious you are to him? *Do you?*"

Do any of us?

THE FACE OF CHRIST IN OTHERS

I believe that when we see even the briefest glimpse of Christ's face, when we hear even the slightest sound of his voice, our soul begins to ache. Sometimes those sights and sounds come to us through the arts—in a movie like *Les Misérables* or a sculpture like Michelangelo's *Pietà*. Most of the time, though, they come to us not so much in the art produced *by us* as much as in the art God is producing *in us*. I'm thinking of the likeness of his Son that he is shaping in all of us, a likeness that in some way reflects the Father's own face.

My brother's face comes to mind. In my brother's face—at some moments, and sometimes for the briefest of moments—I see something of the face of our father,

44

who is no longer with us. From time to time, I see something of Dad's face in the face of my son. That is because the three of us—my brother, my son, and I— all share the same genetic heritage. We who are born into the family of God share a similar heritage—the face of our heavenly Father, which is seen most clearly in the face of his Son.

We don't know what Jesus' face looked like. Here and there, though, we see something of it filtered through the faces of those around us.

A Face on Sunset Boulevard

45

I once saw a reflection of Christ's face in Los Angeles, as diverse a city as there is on the planet, with an equally diverse collection of faces. While attending the City of Angels Film Festival, at the Directors Guild on Sunset Boulevard, I took a walk during a break in the evening schedule to get some fresh air and take in some of the sights on this most legendary of Hollywood streets.

The stroll turned out to be sensory overload. Billboards lined the boulevard with larger-than-life images, looking as if they were mythological gods partying on Mt. Olympus and every so often peering down to earth to see if the mortals were paying them sufficient homage. Each display boasted beautiful people with beautiful bodies in beautiful clothes. Calvin Klein. Gucci. Armani. From suggestive to seductive, they were glitzy and glamorous and impossible to ignore.

"Buy us," they seemed to whisper, "and you will be

e us; you will become one of us, one of the beautiful
ɔds that people look up to, worship, make sacrifices
or."

It was different from a red-light district—not in
kind, only by degree. It was a classier neighborhood,
but the seductions were the same.

Tables and chairs spilled out onto the sidewalks
beneath umbrellas offering shelter to the "almost
famous" who had gathered for martinis or mineral
water, salads or some other low-fat fare. Like billboards
come to life, they were impossible to ignore. Beautiful
people with beautiful bodies in beautiful clothes—the
women holding on desperately to their youth, and
some with a white-knuckled grip on it.

How much makeup, I wondered, *makes all this possible? How many manicures and facial peels, how many
trips to the tanning salon, how much plastic surgery?*

The gods must be pleased with the sacrifices.

After a few blocks, I began to feel like an outsider,
as anonymous as a haggard street person in threadbare
clothes. No one turned to look. No one smiled. No
one said a word. At least not to me.

When I finally returned to the Directors Guild,
I slipped into a small theater where a short film about
capital punishment was slated to be shown. Only a
sprinkling of people were in the audience as I sank into
a cushioned seat. Behind me sat a young nun—how
young it was difficult to say: twenty-five, thirty-five,
maybe even late thirties.

She wore no designer clothes, just a crisply pressed,
sky-blue habit, bordered in white. Her hair was not

styled. In fact, it was completely covered. I had no idea
even what color it was. Most likely, she hadn't had her
face lifted, hadn't had anything implanted or removed
or straightened or injected. She wasn't wearing makeup
or jewelry.

One other thing: She was radiant.

I am not a person who normally strikes up conversations with strangers, but her appearance was such a
striking contrast to the people I had just seen on Sunset Boulevard that I felt compelled. I don't recall ever
talking with a nun before, and I have to admit I felt
a bit awkward. I'm married, and she of course was not,
which added to the awkwardness.

I smiled and said hi. She smiled back. I stumbled
into the conversation by asking her about her uniform,
if the color had any particular meaning. No, she said,
that was just what they wore in the warmer months.
In the cooler seasons, they wore black.

"When did you become a nun?" I asked.

"When I was seventeen."

"What made you want to become one?" I asked.
Her face lit up, and she smiled. "God got a hold of me
and changed my life."

She told me something of her spiritual journey, and
I listened, totally enthralled. As she talked, I saw something of Jesus in her face, something of his love, his joy.
And suddenly I didn't feel so much like someone lost
in a sprawling city, but rather as one who had just been
shown the way home.

It's easy to get lost in Los Angeles, so when I arrived
there, I had purchased a *Thomas Guide*, which is a

multipage, spiral-bound map that lists the street names in its index and cross-references them by page number to a grid. H-6, for example. Or B-13. Even if you've never read a map in your life, you can pinpoint where you want to go.

But what if Sunset Boulevard . . . or Rodeo Drive . . . or Avenue of the Stars is not where you want to go? What if it's another kingdom you're looking for? Not the Magic Kingdom of Disneyland, but the kingdom that Jesus talked about, which, of all kingdoms, is not only the most real but the most magical. Where do you go to find such a place? What coordinates do you look for?

You look in the face of someone who loves him. Someone who *really* loves him. Someone who has left everything to follow him. Someone who has seen his face, perhaps in the face of the poor, and who is radiant in the reflection.

The glow is not the result of cosmetics or chemical peels or clothes whose colors bring out one's complexion.

The glow is that of the moon as it beholds the sun.

Of all the faces I saw that weekend, both on the silver screen and on Sunset Boulevard, none looked as fair and as pure as the face of the nun at the Directors Guild. And none was as clear in providing direction.

A Face Halfway around the World

As the young nun and I were talking, a dark-skinned man who appeared to be from India sat down one seat removed from hers. I was telling her that several of my favorite writers were Catholic. I mentioned that there were three people I had wanted to meet before I died, and two of them were Catholic: Mother Teresa and Henri Nouwen. Unfortunately, both had already died, and I expressed my regret at not having met them.

"I once met Henri Nouwen," she said, "at a book signing." I asked about him, and she told me he was kind and humble and soft-spoken, a very unpretentious man, and that she had enjoyed his writing, too. When she finished, the man next to her spoke.

"And I have met Mother Teresa," he said.

My eyes lit up. "Really? Tell me about her."

He told us he had met her several years ago. As part of her daily routine, she received visitors between ten and eleven o'clock each morning, and the visitors were allowed to follow her as she made her rounds. The day he met her, she was trailing behind the doctors who were treating the bedridden patients that she cared for. The doctors touched the patients they examined, some of whom had serious and communicable diseases, but their hands were protected by latex gloves. Mother Teresa, he told us, wore no gloves. With her bare, wrinkled hands, she affectionately touched the hands and arms and faces of these most desperately ill people. As she talked with them or prayed with them, she tenderly rubbed her hands over their withered skin.

"What was it like, being there with her?" I asked.

He paused a moment and smiled. "It was like being in the presence of Christ."

"I never met anyone more memorable" than Mother Teresa, writes Malcolm Muggeridge, a British journalist who had interviewed in his career a legion

49

of memorable people. "Just meeting her for a fleeting moment makes an ineffaceable impression. I have known people burst into tears when she goes, though it was only from a tea party where their acquaintance with her amounted to no more than receiving her smile."

In a slender, unassuming biography he wrote, titled *Something Beautiful for God,* Muggeridge describes his first meeting with Mother Teresa, which was an interview for the BBC in London. As he waited for her to arrive, he sat in a room where the interview was to be held, brushing up on his notes, coming up with more questions to ask, and making sure the camera, lights, and sound equipment were all in place. "Then," he explains, "she came in. It was, for me, one of those special occasions when a face, hitherto unknown, seems to stand out from all other faces as uniquely separate and uniquely significant, to be thenceforth forever recognizable."

Muggeridge was so intrigued by Mother Teresa that he traveled to India and followed the slightly built, stooped-over nun and many of her coworkers as they went about their daily routines. In his book *Jesus: The Man Who Lives,* he explains the effect the experience had on him: "In the dismal slums of Calcutta, Mother Teresa and her Missionaries of Charity go about Jesus's work of love with incomparable dedication. When I think of them, as I have seen them at their work and at their devotions, I want to put away all the books, tear up all the scribbled notes. There are no more doubts or dilemmas; everything is perfectly clear. What commen-

tary or exposition, however eloquent, lucid, perceptive,
inspired even, can equal in elucidation and illumina-
tion the effect of these dedicated lives? What mind
has conceived a discourse, or tongue spoken it, which
conveys even to a minute degree the light they shine
before men? *I was an hungred, and ye gave me meat;
I was thirsty, and ye gave me drink: I was a stranger,
and ye took me in: naked and ye clothed me: I was sick,
and ye visited me: I was in prison, and ye came unto
me*—the words come alive, as no study or meditation
could possibly make them, in the fulfillment in the
most literal sense of Jesus's behest to see in the suffering face of humanity his suffering face, and in their
broken body, his. The religion Jesus gave the world is
an experience, not a body of ideas or principles. It is in
being lived that it lives, as it is in loving that the love
which it discloses at the heart of all creation becomes
manifest. . . . In the face of a Mother Teresa I trace the
very geography of Jesus's Kingdom; all the contours
and valleys and waterways. I need no other map."

After his first television interview with Mother
Teresa, Muggeridge described the effect it had on him
and his viewers, which led him to a moment of reflection. "Discussions are endlessly taking place about
how to use a mass medium like television for Christian
purposes, and all manners of devices are tried, from
dialogues with learned atheists and humanists to pop
versions of the psalms and psychedelic romps. Here
was the answer. Just get on the screen a face shining
and overflowing with Christian love; someone for
whom the world is nothing and the service of Christ

51

everything; someone reborn out of servitude to the ego and the flesh, and into the glorious liberty of the children of God. Then it doesn't matter how the face is lighted or shot; whether in front or profile, close-up or two-shot or long-shot; what questions are put, or by whom. The message comes over . . . the same message that was heard in the world for the first time two thousand years ago; as Mother Teresa showed, it has not changed its sense or lost its magic."

There is something in a face that reflects the love of Christ. Something good and beautiful, to be sure. But something else. Something *true,* the way true north is true.

Muggeridge was right. In the face of someone who loves Jesus we *can* trace the very geography of his kingdom.

All the contours and valleys and waterways.

We need no other map.

Seeing what I saw in the face of the nun at the Directors Guild, and in the faces along Sunset Boulevard, makes me wonder what others see in mine. If some road-weary person were to look into my face, would he find all the lush contours, all the lilied valleys, all the life-giving waterways of Christ's kingdom?

Or would he need another map?

Transformed by a Face

Thomas Dubay, in his book *The Evidential Power of Beauty,* tells a story about a teenage girl in the atheistic Soviet Union who knew nothing of the Bible, nothing of the doctrines of the church, nothing of the differences between denominations. She also knew nothing of Jesus. Until one day she chanced upon a copy of Luke's Gospel. When she finished reading it, her immediate reaction was, "I fell in love with him."

Isn't that beautiful?

"I fell in love with him."

Isn't that what reading the Bible should do to us? Isn't that what going to church should do to us, what being in ministry should do to us, what studying in seminary should do to us?

Then why so often doesn't it?

During my first semester in seminary, I heard a professor say something that has haunted me ever since. He was one of the most respected professors on the faculty, and what he said was this: "Stay away from the third- and fourth-year students." Why? Because, we were told, they were critical and bitter, and being around them would destroy our passion.

Pretty sobering. At the time I heard those words, I thought that maybe the seminary, like some collegiate athletic program, had simply had a couple of bad recruiting years and that things would eventually turn around for them. Maybe our class would turn things around. I later learned that the professor gave the same warning each year to every class of first-year students.

That was even more sobering. And confusing. Why was this happening? And why was it continuing to happen, year after year? We were reading the same book the Russian teenager had read. So why weren't *we* falling more in love with Jesus?

For lots of reasons, I suppose. Perhaps as many

53

reasons as there were students. But one of the reasons, I believe, is this: We are not transformed by a curriculum; we are transformed by a person. And we are transformed not by studying that person but by beholding him. Busyness is not conducive to beholding. And, because seminary life is above all a busy life, perhaps that explains, at least partly, why falling in love with Jesus doesn't happen there as often as it should.

A lot of busyness stems from individual and corporate efforts aimed at helping people get over their struggles so they can go on to maturity. In *The Pursuit of God,* A. W. Tozer describes what I believe is a better model: "The man who has struggled to purify himself and has had nothing but repeated failures will experience real relief when he stops tinkering with his soul and looks away to the perfect One. While he looks at Christ, the very things he has so long been trying to do will be getting done within him. It will be God working in him to will and to do."

Love changes us in ways that law cannot. Spiritual formation, a term used to describe the process of being changed into the image of Christ, doesn't happen by following disciplines. It happens by falling in love. When we fall in love with Jesus, all the other loves in our life fall into place. And those that once competed with Christ now subordinate themselves to him. Everything in our life finds its proper value once we have properly valued him.

We take time for what we value. And we behold what we love. It is not the duty of beholding that changes us, though, but rather the beauty of the one

54

we behold. When Christ at last appears, we will behold him not only in all his beauty but for all eternity. And we will be like him, John says, because we will see him for the first time as he really is (see 1 John 3:2).

One day we *will* be transformed. And it will be a face that transforms us. Here on this earth it is also a face that transforms us, though here we see it through a glass darkly, often distortedly, and only fleetingly (see 1 Corinthians 13:12).

That is why busyness is lethal—it keeps us from beholding the face of Jesus. And that is why stillness is essential—to get the best possible look at his face, for the longest possible time.

55

Beholding Christ's face is the still point of the dance, around which all our activity should revolve.

If that is not the still point in our lives, there is no dance.

There is only movement.

THE JOY
OF THE DANCE

*"Dance is more than just steps. Feel the music
and just dance for sheer joy."*

There's a heartbreaking moment in the Japanese film *Shall We Dance?* where a dance instructor working with a beginning student berates him in front of the class: "Stop. Control yourself. Slobbering like that. Your hands are dripping wet. You're making me sick. There's no way you're becoming my partner."

Imagine what it must have felt like to hear those words hurled with such fierceness, to see those eyes glaring with such disgust. Here was an awkward, disheveled man with no sense of rhythm, wanting so much to dance that he braved taking a beginning class; who put himself out there on the dance floor, where week after week he exposed his clumsiness to everyone.

The slump-shouldered man is so humiliated by the attack that he can hardly look the instructor in the face. He takes a step back, staring at the floor in a moment of shame-filled silence. Then somehow he finds the courage to look up and speak: "Do I really make you sick? Am I really that disgusting? Do I really look that bad?"

Now imagine that this scene is not one from a movie but a scene from real life. Imagine that you're the clumsy one who has just been shamed. Would you stay for the rest of the class? Would you ever come back? Maybe if you could get another instructor. Or maybe you'd just find another class somewhere else.

Maybe.

More likely, you would give it all up—not only the trying but also the dreaming. You would give up the fantasy that there was a place for you somewhere on the dance floor; that there was a partner for you out there, waiting to take your hand.

How would you feel about dancing with someone who looked at you with such disgust? How would anyone feel?

We might work with someone like that, by necessity, but we would never dance with such a person. Or if we did, it would be to gain the person's approval, attention, or acceptance. But that's not dancing. That's performing. Dancing is more than getting the steps right. It's about feeling the music and moving to the music. It's about losing ourselves in the embrace of someone we love. Above all, it's about joy.

There is satisfaction in getting the steps right. There is a thrill in the grand, sweeping movements of the dance. There is something gratifying about the acknowledgment of others. And yet . . .

The joy of the dance is not in the precision of our steps.

It's not in the exhilaration of being swept away.

It's not in the affirmation of the audience.

60

The joy of the dance is in the delight in our partner's eyes.

The dance of intimacy is more than just steps. It's about being in the Lord's arms as we follow his steps, close enough to his heart that we feel the music. It's not about just being swept away, however good that feels. It's about being swept away *by him.* It's not about what others think of us; it's about what *he* thinks. And what he thinks is captured in his eyes.

If we feel detachment in those eyes, we won't dance. If we feel disapproval, we won't dance. If we feel disgust, we won't dance. We won't even take the first step.

But if we feel detachment, disapproval, or disgust, it is really just a projection of our own self-image— not how Jesus feels about us. Because when Jesus looks at us, no matter how we feel about ourselves, he feels *delight.*

And that delight is in his eyes before we ever take our first step, just as the delight that God the Father had for his Son was in his eyes before Jesus took his first step. On the day of Christ's baptism, a proud Father spoke out: "This is my Son, chosen and marked by my love, delight of my life" (Matthew 3:17, *The Message*). The Father delighted in Jesus *before* he died on the cross. He delighted in Jesus *before* he made his first disciple, *before* he preached his first sermon, *before* he performed his first miracle. Why? Because Jesus was his Son.

If you've ever had a child, you know.

The delight is there long before the first step.

The pictures I saw of Jesus when I was a child were mostly stoic, devoid of extremes. I didn't see delight in his eyes, at least not in those portraits. There was neither joy nor sorrow, laughter nor tears, elation nor depression. His expression was somewhere safely in the middle. Similar to the way he was portrayed physically—not quite a Jew yet not quite a Gentile, either. Somewhere in between.

The picture of him I remember most was an eight-by-ten-inch portrait framed on a wall in our home. His skin was smooth and tan. His hair silken and brown. His posture stately. His features airbrushed to perfection. His head was turned slightly to one side, eyes looking away, almost as if he had been posed by a photographer who told him not to look at the camera.

As a kid who got into my share of mischief, snitching cookies from the cupboard or sneaking loose change from my mother's purse, I was glad his eyes looked away.

I remember one picture, though, where his eyes didn't look away. While on vacation in California, our family visited a chapel where a picture of Jesus was the main attraction. We filed reverently into the wooden pews of the small room, and as the lights dimmed, we watched the arched doors in front of us slowly open, revealing a huge portrait of Christ.

What was remarkable about the portrait were the eyes.

Wherever you sat, the eyes looked at you. Not only

at you but *through* you. Or so it seemed to me as a young boy with plenty inside I didn't want him seeing. And if that weren't spooky enough, if you stood up to walk around the room, the eyes followed you. I never knew how they did it. I still don't. But I still remember those eyes following me with their unblinking scrutiny.

I saw different things in the eyes of those portraits.

I saw detachment. I saw disappointment.

What I never saw was delight.

I have another picture I want to share with you, one that I stumbled across in the library of a Catholic retreat center.

I was scheduled to speak on a Saturday to a pastoral staff in Michigan. Arriving the day before, I was housed overnight at the retreat center where the all-day seminar was to be held. As it happened, I was the only one staying there. Except for the few who worked there, I had the place to myself.

Which brought out the kid in me.

The conclave of buildings was built out of white chalky stone with tall monkish windows and richly grained woodwork. The chapel had stained glass. The polished linoleum floors led down narrow corridors that brought me to a dormitory of small, sparsely furnished rooms.

Once I unpacked, I walked outside. The trees and hedges muffled the sounds of the city. The grounds were well kept, budding and fragrant. A stark contrast to the long, dry season that was my spiritual life. It was a refreshing change in scenery. I didn't think, didn't pray, just wandered from place to place, breathing it all in.

The walk did me good.

Until I started thinking about the next day.

I felt so unprepared. Not in terms of the material I was presenting. In terms of me. God seemed so distant. And I had grown so weary of trying to figure out why.

It seemed less as if I were at a dance and more as if I were the last one to leave the dance, stranded there without a ride. And as one might call out over the empty dance floor to see if anyone else was there, my prayers had a hollow echo to them. Why is God so silent at times when you most want him to speak, most *need* him to speak? A word would mean so much. Even if it were a harsh word. It's no word at all that is so difficult to endure.

In my stroll around the property, I came across some kind of shrine, made of various size rocks, cemented together, not at all like the carefully masoned stone of the retreat center. On the walls of the alcove, a few icons had been placed. In the center stood a concrete table, looking something like an altar. On the altar sat a glass fishbowl, filled with folded-up pieces of paper.

Almost irresistibly, I was attracted to it. Was I drawn by boyish curiosity? Or was I *led*?

I looked to my right, then to my left, to see if anyone was watching. Assured no one was, I reached into the bowl and pulled out one of the pieces of paper. The words were something like, "Thank you for the woman our son is marrying. I pray for the wedding, that all would go well . . ."

So this is what this is, I thought to myself, *a prayer shrine.*

I looked right, then left.

Replacing the first prayer, I pulled out another.

"Please help us raise the money we need for the church's furnace . . ."

Fairly simple prayers. Nothing to get all that excited about. I felt silly, standing there reading them—like a little kid sneaking cookies, taking a bite out of each one and putting it back until I found one I liked.

Looking right, looking left.

Putting the cookie back, reaching for another.

"Dear God, please don't let anyone in the church find out about what I did . . ."

The cookies were getting better.

The prayer never mentioned what he didn't want the church to find out. One could only imagine. Which I did.

Looking right, then left.

Reaching for another, digging deeper, until this one:

Dear God,

Please grant me your strength.
I am weak and tired. I cannot find you.
Please, for your love, reveal yourself.

I love you,

He had signed his full name.

Tears filled my eyes. My face flushed, not because I was reading someone else's prayer, but because I was reading my own. I felt such compassion for the man. I prayed for him, prayed for myself, then left.

Later that night, after all the staff had gone home, I walked the high-gloss floors. The soles of my shoes echoed off the walls. I felt like a kid in some other family's house, left alone for the night, knowing none of the family would be back until tomorrow, and so there was no fear of being found out, no fear of being caught someplace where I didn't belong. A boyish excitement bubbled within me.

I stopped in the stainless steel kitchen, its sheen dulled from years of meals that had been prepared there. I opened the cupboards, looking for something to eat, a late-night snack. Peanut butter. *Well, that's a start.* I eased open the refrigerator door. A jar of grape jelly, who knows how old, stood on the rack. Turning the lid, I looked inside. *Nothing growing in it.* A good sign. Half a loaf of bread lay next to it. Nothing growing there, either.

And we have a sandwich!

I don't remember enjoying a sandwich more. Peanut butter and jelly sandwiches were one of the sacraments of my childhood. And for a few moments, something of the happy days of my youth came back to me. To be a kid again, if only for a day. A kick-back, carefree kid. A kid who was looked after and loved. Who was tucked in and told stories. Who was given peanut butter sandwiches washed down with whole milk.

I checked the refrigerator. A lonely gallon of milk cowered in the back. I checked the expiration date. Not trusting it, I twisted the cap and brought my nose to the opening. Not trusting my sense of smell, I poured a glass and tipped it toward my mouth.

It passed inspection, and now I had something to wash down the peanut butter.

Finishing the snack, I wandered the halls again. This time I came to a library with floor-to-ceiling bookshelves and a number of cozy seating areas grouped together. I browsed the shelves. I saw a CD player on the window seat and a collection of CDs shelved neatly next to it. Thinking I would find something like a ten-volume set of Gregorian chants, sung without accompaniment, I was surprised by what I saw on top of the stereo.

67

Simon and Garfunkel. *Greatest Hits.*

Ever since high school, Simon and Garfunkel had been my favorite singers. I had seen them in concert in 1969, and before I left California in 1993, my wife and I went to a concert by Art Garfunkel. I put the headphones on and listened. "Bridge Over Troubled Water" was the first song. Such a great song. And such a great illustration of Jesus being the friend who laid himself down as a bridge over the troubled waters of sin that separated us from God.

The effect that moment had on me is difficult to describe. It seemed a sudden and unexpected breeze, cool and refreshing. Finding the Simon and Garfunkel CD heightened my anticipation as to what else might be there in that old library. I walked around, looking with new eyes at the surroundings. I paused over the pictures on the walls. One by one I looked at them, not knowing what I might discover in them, or they in me.

The next picture was a painting of Jesus. He was standing, dressed in a rust-colored robe, open in the front, revealing a white garment underneath. A halo circled his head. His brownish hair had a tint of red, picking up the color of the robe. I looked at the face. It was not the golden-brown face of the portrait of Jesus that is so common. The skin was whiter. It was the artist's effort to pick up the white in the undergarment to give the picture a stronger sense of composition. The color started at the bottom of the frame, extending to the face and the halo, which almost touched the top of the frame. I stared at the face, studying its features.

Then I saw it.

The whitish skin.

The reddish hair.

The structure of the face.

The shape of the eyes.

It looks like me.

Not exactly like me, certainly. But lose the halo, cut the hair, shave the beard, put on some bifocals, add twenty years, and there was a definite resemblance.

The face in the picture was serious but not sad. The eyes were soft, not in the least bit reproachful. The hands were poised not in an accusatory gesture but in a revelatory one.

I looked at his mouth, but the lips were closed. He was saying nothing. Yet his hands were poised as if he were wanting to say something. One hand was held horizontally. The other, vertically. *Did the artist capture him at the moment after he had spoken,* I wondered, *or at the moment just before?*

If the picture could speak, what would it say?

If I were standing before Jesus himself, instead of simply an artist's portrayal, what would he say? I mean, to me.

I halfway expected the lips to move—which, of course, they didn't.

As I reflected on the experience and what God might be saying through it, I realized that all the questions I had about what he was doing in my life were answered in that picture. He was at work in my life, making me more like his Son.

God had indeed been silent. But silent in the way an artist at work is silent. He had been quietly at work in me, forming Christ in me.

It is the last place we look when we are looking to see Jesus.

In ourselves.

It is certainly the last place *I* would look.

We are told in the Scriptures that one day we will be "like Him" (1 John 3:2). It seems a destiny too incredible to imagine, let alone to credibly believe, but we are told that this is not only our destiny in the hereafter but that God is using the here-and-now circumstances of our lives to begin the process (see Romans 8:29-39).

If this is true, we are works in progress on our way to becoming masterpieces. However rough the sketch appears, a painting of incomparable beauty is emerging from it. If the work is progressing, it stands to reason that we should see something of that beauty emerging in our lives. We should look different, even

69

to ourselves, than we did ten years ago; look more like Christ than we did then, think more like him, feel more like him, sound more like him. Hopefully, if the work is progressing, we should look different than we did five years ago, different from a year ago, a month ago, maybe even a few hours ago.

It is hard, perhaps impossible, to be objective when we talk about ourselves. At least it is for me. Adding to the difficulty, I don't *like* to talk about myself. Part of that, I'm sure, is the little boy in me who, for some reason or another, never grew up and who maybe doesn't want to grow up and consequently feels uncomfortable in the presence of others who have. Part of the reason, I'm also sure, is that I know who I am. I know the person behind the nicely worded sentences that some people seem to like. I know that he doesn't always think nicely worded sentences to himself or say very nicely worded sentences to others sometimes. I know the dark places within him where very bad thoughts work very hard at coming up with those words.

I am out of touch with a lot of things, but my sin is not one of them.

Because I am perhaps more in touch with the sin at work in me than I am sometimes with the grace that is also at work in me, the conversations I have with myself about myself are often not ones I would want others to hear. I say terrible things to myself sometimes. Things I know that Jesus would never say—never think to say even.

All this to say that seeing the good in me and talking about the good, objectively, doesn't come easy. So what did I see in that painting of Christ hanging on the library wall in a retreat center where I was the only overnight guest?

I saw kindness.

I have experienced much kindness in my life, both from other people and from God. The kindness of God leads us to repentance, Paul says in Romans 2:4, and I would say that, too. It has led me there many times and doubtless will lead me there many times again. But it has also led me to other places—to humility, which I guess is a part of repentance, maybe even at the heart of it. The kindness of God has led me also to love. And to gratefulness. And to peace. And generosity. And kindness to others, even to myself.

I have great tenderness in my heart for people to whom the world has shown little kindness—people, especially children, who have mental or physical handicaps or who in some way or another don't fit in and are left on the outside, feeling very lonely and bad about themselves. I naturally gravitate to such people. I don't think about it beforehand, nor do I pat myself on the back about it afterward, but those are the people I want to talk with when I am at a small social gathering or at a large speaking engagement. It is their eyes I want to make contact with. It is their heart I want to touch and their heart I want to touch mine. I want them to feel something of how they might feel if Jesus were there instead of me. I want them to feel the love he would feel for them. I want them to feel how precious they are to him, how dear the very sound of their name is to his ears. I want to listen to them the way he would listen, and communicate to them by my listening that their stories matter, their pain matters, *they* matter.

I think of Jesus and the people he gravitated toward, and it wasn't the rich or the powerful, the intelligent or the beautiful, the gifted or the influential. By and large, it was just the opposite. He had a tender heart for the hurting, and gravitated toward them. Whether the hurt was physical, mental, spiritual, emotional, moral, social, or relational, it didn't seem to matter. He was always kind to them, to each and every one of them.

It is the part of me most like Christ. And the part of me I most like. But I never really thought about it until I saw that picture of Christ in the library.

In it I saw something of myself. Through it I saw something of his delight.

I have one more picture. This one graces the palace of a king, unfolded for us in scenes, like a mural, revealing a tonal portrait of a man's love for his bride. The mural is titled "The Song of Solomon." As you listen to some of Solomon's words, imagine yourself as the love of his life, looking into his eyes as he looks into yours.

"You have made my heart beat faster, my sister, my bride. You have made my heart beat faster with a single glance of your eyes." SONG OF SOLOMON 4:9

"O my dove . . . let me see your form, let me hear your voice; for your voice is sweet, and your form is lovely."

SONG OF SOLOMON 2:14

"How beautiful and how delightful you are, my love."
SONG OF SOLOMON 7:6

If the allegory holds true, that is the way Jesus feels about *us*. We can see it in his eyes. It's not disgust. It's not disapproval. It's not detachment.

It's delight.

"To be loved by God," said C. S. Lewis, "not merely pitied, but delighted in as an artist delights in his work or a father in a son—it seems impossible," but that is the picture of God we see in the Scriptures. If that's the picture we have, it will change not only the way we see ourselves, it will change the way we see everything. Including the Scriptures. Now as I read them, I try not only to hear what the people heard but to see what they saw.

73

I imagine, for example, looking at Jesus through the eyes of the hemorrhaging woman he meets in Mark 5:34. After his eyes had picked her out of the crowd as the one who touched him, she fell at his feet, trembling. When he said, "Daughter, your faith has made you well; go in peace, and be healed of your affliction," I'm sure she looked up at him. And I try to imagine what she saw in his eyes.

Was it a far-off look? an accusatory arch of the eyebrow? a look of repulsion?

I don't think so. I think she saw delight. I think she saw his pleasure in her faith, however brief the touch of her hand, however feeble the grasp on his garment.

Seeing the delight in Christ's eyes is what will

entice us onto the dance floor. It's what will give us the courage to take that first, tentative step. It's what will start us dancing. It's also what will *keep* us dancing.

THE MUSIC
OF THE DANCE

"I need the music to get me to dance."

VIOLETTE VERDY

Violette Verdy was a twelve-year-old prodigy in 1945, studying ballet in Paris, when she was offered a contract to dance professionally. She later joined the New York City Ballet, where she spent most of her career. In spite of her natural gifting, in spite of her professional training, in spite of her extensive experience, she needed something else. "I need the music to get me to dance," she acknowledged. "I need it to give me the strength, the courage, the conviction, the desire, the pleasure, the emotion."

I need the music, too. I need it in different ways on different days. On some days, I need it for strength. On others, for courage. On still others, for conviction. I need it on some days to help me believe that the life I am living is indeed a dance and not just random acts of clumsiness. Some days, I'm just too tired and feel I can't keep up anymore. On those days especially I need the music to get me to dance.

Dancing seems to come naturally to all my children, three girls and a boy, each of whom is a good dancer, one of whom is majoring in it and wants to make a career of it. I'm not sure where they got the ability—their mother, most likely—but I do know where they didn't get it. From me. Dancing does not come naturally to me, either in the physical or the spiritual realm, and whatever rhythmic genes I might have passed on from my side of the family were recessive in me.

Years ago, when our children were much younger, Tim Scott, who played Mephistopheles in the Broadway production of *Cats,* spent Christmas day with us and a close friend of ours. After lunch I asked Tim if he would teach the kids some dance steps. He lined them up, demonstrated a few basic moves, then picked some music for them to dance to. At first they were all out of step. While they were looking to him for direction, he was graciously coaching them, but still they weren't getting it. Then he said something that changed everything. "Feel the music," he said. And when they did, their moves became more natural, more in sync, not only with the music but also with themselves.

I think there's something to that in the spiritual realm. Some kind of correlation between feeling the music and falling in step. When we all feel the music, our movements seem to be in sync not only with the music but with each other.

We feel the music of the dance when Jesus' longing for us and our longing for him meet in a moment of embrace, which is not only a transcendent moment but one that often evokes tears.

Those moments come spontaneously. They can't be scheduled. Or manipulated. Or coerced. They are, after all, moments of grace. And grace is given. It is always given, never taken. That grace may come through a moment in the Scriptures . . . or through a moment in the theater. It may come through an inarticulate moment with a homeless person on the street . . . or through an eloquent moment in the Chronicles of Narnia that you're reading to your granddaughter who's snuggled next to you.

Those moments may come anytime, anywhere. But they seem to come most often, at least for me, through music.

My taste in music is eclectic, ranging from classical to country. I could listen to Russell Watson singing lyrics from an Italian opera, not understand a word of it, yet be totally swept away. I could sit by the clear country brook that is Willie Nelson's voice and listen to him sing about anything, whether it's something as simple as "Blue Skies" or as emotionally complex as "My Heroes Have Always Been Cowboys."

When Nelson once said that "all music is sacred because life is sacred," I think I understand what he meant. Even the sadness of a country song is sacred. Maybe *especially* the sadness. But like life itself, sadness is not all there is to the songs that chronicle our sacred journeys. There is love, too. And joy. I'm thinking of the John Michael Montgomery song "I Love the Way You Love Me," a song he sings to the woman he loves.

"I love the way you love me," Montgomery sings. "Strong and wild. Slow and easy. Heart and soul. So completely."

It is the way Jesus loves us, I think.

Strong and wild, as in the way he calmed storms
and cast out demons. In the dramatic way he stilled
the raging waters that have washed over the bows of
all of our lives at some time or another. In the decisive
way he dealt with the inner demons in us all that once
threatened to destroy us and those we love.

Slow and easy, as in the way he taught on prayer.
The disciples, wondering where Jesus went during the
wee hours of the morning. Watching him from a
distance, overhearing fragments of his prayers. And
Jesus, all the while wanting to teach them, but willing
to wait until they asked.

Heart and soul, his eyes brimming with compassion
over the brokenness he saw, his own heart broken over
Jerusalem, over the crowd that mocked him, over the
soldiers that crucified him, over the world that rejected
him.

So completely, giving his life, not a voluntary tithe
of it or even a large, professional portion of it. It was
his life he gave. *His whole life.*

One of the lines of Montgomery's song is "I like
the feel of your name on my lips." Somehow the
name *Jesus* feels different on my lips than the word
Christ or *Lord.* I can't explain why, it just does. Maybe it's because it sounds less theological and more
personal—because it's his name instead of his title.
I remember a time at a conference, singing the song
"Holy and Anointed One," each chorus growing
louder as the congregation sang, almost as if the song
had taken on a life of its own. By the third chorus or
so, the words "Jesus, I love you" sent tears streaming

down my face. And I found myself standing with a taste of heaven on my lips, wishing the song would never end.

In his sermon titled "The Weight of Glory," C. S. Lewis describes what I believe happened to me in that moment. "The books or the music in which we thought the beauty was located will betray us if we trust to them; it was not *in* them, it only came *through* them, and what came through them was longing."

What I experienced that day, as I reflect on it, was not simply a great song, or a talented worship leader, or a heady mix of crowd dynamics that frothed up a moment of mass spiritual intoxication. I believe that brief moment of ecstasy, where my longing for Jesus grew more and more intense, was a lifting of the bridal veil, so to speak, when I saw in his eyes the longing he has had for me for all of my life. And everything within me ached to embrace him.

81

Music moves me in ways I can't quite explain.

No theological study about heaven ever made me long for it more than "Somewhere Over the Rainbow," sung by Judy Garland. And when I heard Eva Cassidy's rendition recently, the longing became even more intense.

No book about how to have a good marriage made me long for it as much as "The Prayer," sung by Celine Dion and Andrea Bocelli.

No sermon ever stirred my longing for Christ as

much as the aria "Nessun dorma," sung by Luciano Pavarotti.

C. S. Lewis came closest to explaining the phenomenon in his poem "Vowels and Sirens," in which he speaks of our longings as

> *A music that resembled*
> *Some earlier music*
> *That men are born remembering.*

The human spirit resides in us as a divine instrument with strings tuned to resonate with the rhythms of grace. At times, and often when we least expect it, we catch a few beguiling notes that seem vaguely familiar, though we have never before heard them. Over a period of years, those intermittent notes converge to form musical lines. Over the course of our lives, the lines converge to form themes of a hauntingly beautiful song that we find ourselves longing with all our soul to sing.

C. S. Lewis described the experience well when he said: "All the things that have ever deeply possessed your soul have been but hints of it—tantalizing glimpses, promises never quite fulfilled, echoes that died away just as they caught your ear. But if it should really become manifest—if there ever came an echo that did not die away but swelled into the sound itself—you would know it. Beyond all possibility of doubt you would say 'Here at last is the thing I was made for.'"

I heard such an echo on one of those late-night commercials for musical compilations that are "only available through this special TV offer." The echo came from a musical line in the song "Nessun dorma." I didn't hear the aria in its entirety until a friend gave me a Luciano Pavarotti CD that included it.

The first time I listened to it, I wept. I had no idea why. I didn't understand a word of the lyrics, which were in Italian, so that couldn't explain it. I knew nothing about the story of the opera, so that couldn't explain it. I didn't even know which character in the opera was singing, or why.

I listened to the song over and over that day, turning up the stereo so loud that no other thoughts had a chance to intrude. At the same two places, tears came to my eyes each and every time.

83

The first place was a line of music in the early part of the song that virtually *aches* with longing. The other place was toward the end, where the song picks up the earlier musical line and brings it to an emotional crescendo.

The song begins uneventfully, plodding along with nothing much to distinguish it. Then a musical line is sung with such yearning that it seems the muscle fibers of my heart have been transformed into the strings of some finely tuned instrument, with every one of them trembling in such deep resonance with Pavarotti's voice that I am caught up in his passion.

Then, as suddenly as that strain of music surfaces, it subsides. And with it, the passion. As Pavarotti continues to sing, my heartstrings are still trembling, longing to be reconnected to the passion.

The song moves along, again uneventfully, then pauses.

Filling the pause is the sound of distant voices. In my mind I imagine them to be the voices of angels, calling to those of us on earth who are eagerly waiting for Jesus to return. And they're telling us, "He's coming! Now is the time! Get ready, he's coming!"

With the eyes of my heart, I look up and see Jesus coming down from his throne. At that moment in the aria, the musical line of longing returns. The joy I feel is so intense that my heart can't contain it, and the emotion spills out. The music is now sung more passionately, each note higher—and fuller—than the one before, and I feel everything within me straining to reach Jesus, to embrace him. As the tenor's voice strains at its last note and falls silent in exhaustion, the orchestra picks up the note and carries it even higher.

And I fall silent, exhausted, with tears streaming down my face.

Such longing, Scripture says, is not only at the heart of every human being but at the heart of the entire earth, from animals to plants to the cells that compose them (see Romans 8:18-25). Science now tells us that the entire universe, from supernovas to subatomic particles, is not made up of matter, as was once supposed, but of pockets of energy, which are constantly giving off vibrations. In other words, music is at the heart of the universe. And every structure is tuned to it, every solar system in the galaxy, every cell in our bodies.

As I was listening to "Nessun dorma," it felt as if every cell in my body was in harmony with the heart that lies at the center of the universe. By the end of the song, I loved Jesus more than I did at the beginning, and everything within me seemed to say, "Here at last is the thing I was made for."

A wonderful thing happened to me that day, which I can't deny but can't explain. In *Till We Have Faces,* C. S. Lewis tries to explain the feeling through the experience of one his characters, Psyche. "It was when I was happiest that I longed most. . . . Do you remember? The colour and the smell, and looking across at the Grey Mountain in the distance? And because it was so beautiful, it set me longing, always longing. Somewhere else there must be more of it. Everything seemed to be saying, Psyche come! But I couldn't (not yet) come and I didn't know where I was to come to. It almost hurt me. I felt like a bird in a cage when the other birds of its kind are flying home."

The longing for home is a dominant theme in Lewis's writings. All art is about coming home. All music, all drama, all literature is about coming home. All psychology, too. As well as all theology.

The last part of the book of Revelation talks a lot about that home. It is a place where there is no darkness. No death. No disease. Not even tears. It is a resplendent landscape, with a river of life running through it, and a tree of life growing in it, and the glory of the Lord illumining everything in this bejeweled world that awaits us.

Who wouldn't want Jesus to come back to take us there, and soon?

That is the longing in the words of the last great aria in the Scriptures, found in Revelation 22.

"See, I am coming soon," Jesus calls out, or maybe

sings out, "and my reward is with me, to repay all according to their deeds. I am the Alpha and the Omega, the First and the Last, the Beginning and the End."

And like the distant voices in "Nessun dorma," the Spirit and the Bride of Christ echo their yearning: "Come."

You can feel the emotion in Jesus' voice rising.

"Yes, I am coming soon!"

And you can feel the passion rising in John as his voice reaches a crescendo in response.

"Amen! Come, Lord Jesus!"

Maybe Lewis was right. Maybe the tug we feel when we see a beautiful landscape shimmering in the sunlight or the tears we experience when we hear an enchanting aria reaching its crescendo, maybe what is welling up inside us is the longing we all have for home.

But maybe it is more than that. Maybe it is not so much a longing for home as it is a longing for the One who awaits us there.

Those moments of longing make up the music of the dance. We need that music to get us to dance. We need not just to hear it but also to feel it, and often. If we don't, chances are that whatever dancing we do will be to someone else's tune.

THE FREEDOM
OF THE DANCE

"[He] danced as naturally as a bird flies or a fish swims. By now I knew that I didn't even have to think; I could just give myself to his arm around me with assurance. The guiding arm was so sure and firm, the rhythm such a part of my body now that I could almost forget about my feet."

CATHERINE MARSHALL, *CHRISTY*

The Christian life is about us following Christ's lead, not about him following ours.

He doesn't ask us to write the notes to the music or choreograph the steps to the dance. He asks us merely to take his hand and follow him. To move when he moves. To speed up when he speeds up. To slow down when he slows down. And to stop when he stops.

It is scary living like this; scarier still ministering like this. After all, we are relinquishing the lead.

But look who we're relinquishing it to.

The Emperor.

We shouldn't feel humiliated that we haven't been asked to be the leader.

We should feel honored that we have been asked to be his partner.

Following Christ's lead is dependent on hearing his voice. No writer talks more about that voice than John. That shouldn't surprise us, knowing John and how dear that voice was to him.

In the tenth chapter of his Gospel, John shares his

notes from some of Jesus' teaching on the relationship between hearing and following. The image Jesus uses is that of the shepherd and his sheep. It is similar to the one I am using of the "Emperor Waltz." We are expressing the same truth, I believe, just using different images to do it.

Extending the image, Jesus says that "the sheep hear his voice, and he calls his own sheep by name, and leads them out" (verse 3). The image is one of relationship. The shepherd not only owns the sheep, he knows the sheep. He knows them so well that he has given names to each of them and calls to each of them individually. The relationship he has with them is so personal, so gentle, and so tender that the sheep respond instinctively to his guidance, pricking their ears to the sound of his voice and moving their feet in the direction of his steps.

The shepherd leads the sheep out of their enclosed pen and into open pasture (see verse 9), an image his audience would readily interpret as experiencing life in the freest and fullest way possible (see verse 10).

Eager as the sheep are for pasture, they don't indiscriminately follow any voice that calls to them. They have discernment. They follow a voice they recognize, coming from a person they love, whose leadership they trust (see verse 11). Notice the contrast between their response to the shepherd's voice and the voice of strangers. "When he puts forth all his own, he goes before them, and the sheep follow him because they know his voice." A stranger, on the other hand, has no such relationship with the sheep, and "they simply will not follow, but will flee from him, because they do not know the voice of strangers" (verses 4-5).

The closer the sheep are to the shepherd, the easier it is for them to hear his voice. The longer they remain close, the likelier it is that they will recognize his voice.

If we can't discern the Lord's voice in our life, we will be at the beck and call of every other voice.

The voice of shame, perhaps, from some failure in our past.

The voice of withheld approval, maybe, from a parent or sibling.

The voice of condemnation, from a teacher, possibly, or an employer.

The voice of guilt, from an insatiably dutiful conscience.

The voice of expectation, from the agenda of our peers.

The voice of obligation, from someone else's social calendar.

The voice of need, sometimes urgent, from so many of those around us.

If we have heard from the Savior's own lips how much he loves us and delights in us, it will silence the taunt of voices that put a makeup mirror to our face and point out all the reasons why Jesus couldn't possibly be in love with such a blemished person.

If we have heard from the Savior's own lips what *he* wants from us, it will keep us from feeling bad about turning a deaf ear to the nag of voices all wanting something from us, something maybe that we don't have to give or that the Lord doesn't want us to give, at least for now.

The Lord's voice will quiet many of those voices, however strident. It will calm the others, however insistent. And for those that are in harmony with his voice, it will show us with what part of our lives we should answer them.

———

Although I have felt the Savior's presence over the years, experiencing his love and sensing his leading, the first time I remember hearing his voice was a number of years ago when we lived in southern California.

Late one night, I pulled into the corner 7-Eleven near our house. I made my purchase and as I was coming out, a homeless man approached me, asking for spare change. I dug into my pocket and gave him what I had. He thanked me, and I got in my car. Then, as I put the key in the ignition, I heard a voice.

"Twenty dollars. He needs it."

The words startled me and at the same time confused me. They startled me in the same way the voice in the movie *Field of Dreams* startled Kevin Costner when he first heard the words, "If you build it, he will come." The words came totally out of the blue, yet they were so clear and so specific. They confused me because I didn't have twenty dollars on me to give him. I put the car in reverse and started to back up. Then I heard it again.

"Twenty dollars. He needs it."

For some time, I had been praying to hear God's

voice. *Is this it?* I wondered. It seemed so fragmentary. Suddenly I remembered an envelope at home that had some cash in it. Here was the risk. *If that was indeed God's voice,* I reasoned, *if I don't respond to it, he might not continue the conversation.* I went home, got the twenty dollars, and put it in another envelope.

With great anticipation I drove back to the 7-Eleven, only to find that the mysterious stranger was gone. *That confirms it,* I thought. *It was just some inner voice, arising out of my conscience.* My face flushed with embarrassment. The whole thing seemed so silly now that the man was gone.

Maybe he went to the donut shop around back. That was distinctly my voice thinking those words, not God's. I drove behind the 7-Eleven where the donut shop was located and squinted into the small storefront. The fluorescent lights glared on the glass countertops and display cases, the half-dozen small tables and dozen or so chairs. Then I saw him. He was folded over a cup of coffee, warming his hands around the white Styrofoam.

I didn't want to embarrass him. God knows he'd had plenty of that in his life and didn't need anyone adding to it. So I wrote on a piece of paper something like, "I'm sorry things are so hard. God told me you needed this. God bless you."

I stepped inside the donut shop and handed him the envelope. Not knowing what to say and not wanting to draw attention to him, I said, "I think you dropped this in the parking lot."

As he opened the envelope, I turned and walked out. By the time I had stepped off the sidewalk into the parking lot, he had caught up with me. "Mister," he said. I turned to see two sunken eyes brimming with tears. A few awkward seconds loitered between us, then he touched my arm gently and said, "Thank you."

The tears in his eyes brought the beginning of tears to mine. I touched his arm, nodded, and smiled.

"God bless you," I said.

"God bless you, too."

If I'd had the presence of mind, I would have sat with him, maybe; listened to his story, maybe; done something else to help him, maybe. As it turned out, that was all either of us said. He went back into the donut shop. I went back into my car and drove home.

Who knows what that twenty dollars meant to a man whose only warmth in life came from a Styrofoam cup, whose only shelter came from a donut shop. Maybe it meant only whatever twenty dollars could buy. But maybe it meant more than that. Maybe the man had been praying, as I had, to hear the voice of God, to know that he was real, to know that he cared. Maybe the man needed to know that he mattered to God, the way I needed to know, the way we all need to, especially on some desperate night when we're down on our luck, out on the street, and panhandling for whatever loose change heaven can spare.

94

Commenting on the way Jesus came to earth in the Incarnation and the way he most often comes to us today, Frederick Buechner, in *The Hungering Dark,* writes: "He comes in such a way that we can always turn him down, . . . comes to us in the hungry man we do not have to feed, comes to us in the lonely man we

do not have to comfort, comes to us in all the desperate
human need of people everywhere that we are always
free to turn our backs upon."

Had Jesus come to me that night at the 7-Eleven?

In some way, I believe he had. Of course, I can't
say for sure. And even if I could say for sure, I can't say
why. Was it for me? Was it for the man on the street?
Maybe it was for both of us, who knows for sure?

All I know for sure is this: For a moment in my
largely distracted life, I was fully present to "the sacrament of the present moment," to use Jean-Pierre de
Cassaude's words. I have come to realize that in every
human encounter there are not only gifts to be given
but gifts to be received. And so, at the still point around
which those encounters revolve, I pause to ask Jesus for
the kneeling grace to receive what is offered me and the
knowing grace to give what is asked of me.

At that moment outside the donut shop, I felt as
if I were kneeling at the handrail that separates heaven
from earth, receiving something extended to me from
the generous hand of God. What I received remains,
for the most part, a mystery.

Was it a test? a training exercise? an answer to
prayer?

Or was Jesus simply needing something done, and
I just happened to be the closest one there to do it? Or
perhaps the most willing?

I'm not sure. But I am sure of this: I know I heard
the words. And I know the words were his.

Perhaps that is all I needed to know.

Perhaps that is all we ever need to know.

"Our highest activity," said C. S. Lewis, "must be response, not initiative."

Nowhere is that more clearly illustrated than in the life of Christ. He didn't take the initiative. He only did what he saw the Father doing (see John 5:19). And only said what he heard the Father teach him (see John 8:28; 12:49; 14:10).

John 4–5 shows some examples of his responsiveness. In John 4, Jesus and his disciples are on their way to Jerusalem. Along the way, in Samaria, they stop at a well. While the disciples go into town to get food, Jesus stays at the well. He stays by himself, where he is resting, most likely, because it has been a long journey. But just as likely, he is praying. Perhaps asking the Father what the next step would be. Perhaps listening.

Into that still point of solitude comes a Samaritan woman. Could she be the reason he was drawn there? To that well, that day, that hour? Could she perhaps be the reason he was not only drawn there but drawn to stay there?

On the ground of such a perhaps, Jesus takes a step, drawing her into a dance of words. In the course of their conversation, the Father reveals something to his Son, something about the woman's past that would be pivotal in determining her future (see John 4:16-18).

In that slight but sudden turn of the conversation, the woman is drawn closer. And as thoughts spin in her head, she comes to the dizzying awareness of who this man at the well really is. *The Savior of the world.* That realization sends her reeling toward town to tell everyone she knows. The response is incredible. Throngs of people rush to the well to see for themselves, to hear for themselves, to believe for themselves.

This sweeping turn of events takes the disciples by surprise, and now it is their heads that are dizzy, their thoughts that are spinning. Imagine what the rest of the trip to Jerusalem was like. Imagine the wows and the wide eyes. Imagine the questions. Imagine the anticipation for the next step of the dance.

The next step is recorded in the next chapter, where Jesus and the disciples enter the holy city, stopping at a pool called Bethesda. Patchworks of misery mat the five porches around that pool, stitched together from the frayed ends of the sick, the blind, the lame, and the withered.

So many needs. And such desperate ones. Yet out of all those who so desperately needed a savior, the Savior of the world came to only one of them. With a word, he healed him. But *only* him.

If numbers are the measure of success in the Father's eyes, Samaria was an astounding success and Bethesda an abysmal failure. But the Father never measured his Son by how successful he was, only by how faithful. Fortunately, he measures us the same way (see Matthew 25:14-30).

When the Pharisees caught up with Jesus, they criticized him for working on the Sabbath. His response? "My Father is working until now, and I Myself am working" (John 5:17). When the debate escalated, Jesus told them, "Truly, truly, I say to you, the Son can do nothing of Himself, unless it is something He sees the Father doing; for whatever the Father does, these things the Son also does in like manner" (verse 19).

It was a big dance around the well in Samaria. A small one around the pool of Bethesda. To Jesus, it didn't matter how big the dance was. It only mattered who was dancing there. On that Sabbath day, while everyone else was resting, his Father was the one doing the dancing. And watching him, Jesus joined in. It was a small step in a small dance, but it was the dance the Father was leading him in. For Jesus, that was all that mattered.

Not the size of the dance.

Or the time of the dance.

Or whose toes he would be stepping on.

The intimacy that Jesus had with the Father while he was on earth is the same kind of intimacy Jesus wants to have with us (see John 10:14-16).

What does that look like, I wonder?

What if we only did the things we saw Jesus doing? What if we only spoke the words he taught us? How would that change the way we live? How would it change the way we do ministry?

Okay. Say we did that. Say we drew close to Christ to see what he was doing . . . and we didn't see anything. What then? Say we spent time to hear what he was saying . . . and we didn't hear anything. Say, in some unguarded moment of religious fervor, we vowed to teach only what Christ had taught us . . . and in a sobering moment we realize that he hasn't taught us all that much, at least not personally. What then?

A lot of us would be out of a job.

Or else . . .

Or else we would be into a relationship.

Out of the intimacy of that relationship we may learn to do life differently, to do ministry differently. Who knows what words we will hear there, what things we will see, what feelings we will experience?

Or what freedom?

The freedom of the dance is in following Christ's lead.

He dances so naturally and moves so fluidly that sometimes we don't even have time to think about where he is taking us. Wherever he is taking us, though, there are things he wants to show us along the way, experiences he wants to share with us, words he wants to speak to us. At various turns on the dance floor, there is grace he wants to extend to us . . . and grace he wants to extend *through us* to others.

Our assurance for the guidance we need is not in our education, however excellent it may be. It is not in our experience, however extensive. It is not even in our gifting, however extraordinary. Our assurance is in the arm he has around us. He wants us to feel the firmness of that arm, to trust in its sureness, and to have the music of his voice become such a part of us . . .

that we can almost forget about our feet.

99

THE SPONTANEITY

OF THE DANCE

Don't worry about what you don't know.
Life's a dance.
You learn as you go.

John Michael Montgomery, "Life's a Dance"

L ife with Jesus is a divine dance. But we don't
have to be a dancer, let alone a good one, before
he calls our name, extends his hand, and invites us onto
the dance floor.

He doesn't want us to worry about what we don't
know. He isn't worried. He knows we will learn as
we go.

And that is precisely how we learn—*as we go*. We
learn to dance by dancing. While we are dancing, we
will learn the spontaneity of the dance . . . and we will
learn *to love* the spontaneity.

That won't happen while we are studying the dance.

Not while we are watching others dance.

It will happen *while we are dancing*.

When we take his hand, Jesus will take us places on
the dance floor. Some of them will be exciting places.
Others will be scary. Still others will be puzzling, and
we won't know why he has taken us there. As Jesus
whisks us across the dance floor, sometimes we have
only a blurred remembrance of where he has taken us.

In order to find some pattern in the rhythms, we may need to retrace our steps. I think back on the places Jesus has taken me, the people who brushed by me there, the gifts that were extended to me there, and I begin to see in the steps something of the rhythms of grace.

The following story is about some of those steps and where they led me.

―――――――――――

Of all the books I have in my library, only two authors have shelves of their own.

C. S. Lewis and Frederick Buechner.

C. S. Lewis you know. Frederick Buechner you may not. You pronounce his last name *Beekner,* as he points out somewhere in one of his books. I first came across his name when I was the director for educational products at Insight for Living. Part of my job was to write study guides for the radio ministry of Chuck Swindoll. The other part was to review books to be offered for the ministry's monthly fund-raising appeal. Boxes of books came in every month from various publishers, and my department was responsible to cull through them, review several that might be a good fit for our constituency, and then submit two or three as candidates.

Because I possess a short literary attention span, I read mostly smaller books. For the same reason, I also write smaller books. In one of the many boxes from one of the many publishers, I found *The Sacred Journey* by Frederick Buechner.

I was immediately drawn to it because it was, well, small.

I was also drawn by the title. The words *sacred* and *journey* were not words you often saw in books by Protestants, let alone by Evangelicals. The terms are more prevalent in books by Catholic authors, but here was a Presbyterian using them, not only as his title but also as the central metaphor for his book. This intrigued me.

In the first page of the introduction, Buechner writes: "It seemed to me then, and seems to me still, that if God speaks to us at all in this world, if God speaks anywhere, it is into our personal lives that he speaks."

That was my first moment of resonance with Buechner's work. The words reverberated in my heart because I was at a time in my life when I longed to hear God's voice, not merely in the Scriptures, where I had been trained to hear it, but in the everyday moments of my life, where I was practically illiterate.

The image Buechner uses to describe the process of deciphering those moments is drawn from the Hebrew language, which was particularly intriguing to me because I had been an Old Testament major in seminary. The language of the Old Testament is somewhat elusive because it was originally written only with consonants. The vowels, which were easily deduced by Hebrew readers, were omitted from the text. It wasn't until around A.D. 1000 that a group of Jewish scholars, known as the Masoretes, added vowels to the Old Testament text. Even today, in most written Hebrew, such as a contemporary Jerusalem newspaper, the vowels are absent. It is something like reading a personalized license plate, such as WWIIVT, which most of us would instinctively decipher as "World War II Veteran."

"Like the Hebrew alphabet," Buechner writes, "the alphabet of grace has no vowels, and in that sense his words to us are always veiled, subtle, cryptic, so that it is left to ourselves to delve their meaning, to fill in the vowels for ourselves by means of all the faith and imagination we can muster. God speaks to us in such a way, presumably, not because he chooses to be obscure but because, unlike a dictionary word whose meaning is fixed, the meaning of an incarnate word is the meaning it has for the one it is spoken to, the meaning that becomes clear and effective in our lives only when we ferret it out for ourselves."

For the next hundred or so pages, Buechner goes on to ferret out the voice of God along the barefoot path of his growing up years that begins with his birth in 1926 and ends with his decision to attend seminary in 1953. Other of his books, namely *Now and Then, Telling Secrets,* and *The Longing for Home,* chronicle his days in seminary, his years as a husband and father, and where he is today as a writer and grandfather. These books have been good company on my spiritual journey.

C. S. Lewis once said that we read to know we are not alone. Of course, we read for other reasons as well—for information, for understanding, for guidance, for escapism, for beauty. At the heart of it, though, I think Lewis was right. I think we read to know we are not alone. To know that someone else is out there who shudders from some of the same fears, who struggles with some of the same insecurities, lives with some of the same guilt, broods over some of the same doubts, shares some of the same secrets.

In the third installment of his memoirs, Buechner writes: "I have called this book *Telling Secrets* because I have come to believe that by and large the human family all has the same secrets, which are both very telling and very important to tell. They are telling in the sense that they tell what is perhaps the central paradox of our condition—that what we hunger for perhaps more than anything else is to be known in our full humanness, and yet that is often just what we also fear more than anything else."

He goes on to say that telling our secrets makes it easier for others to tell theirs, which is what a family should be about, especially the family of God. He concludes his introduction by stating: "Finally, I suspect that it is by entering that deep place inside us where our secrets are kept that we come perhaps closer than we do anywhere else to the One who, whether we realize it or not, is of all our secrets the most telling and the most precious we have to tell."

The secrets we have to tell are not just the cowering secrets that have closeted themselves in our innermost selves, but the childlike ones that are eager to throw open the front door and run out to play. Our sorrows are not the only secrets we keep. Our joys are often kept carefully guarded, too, especially our joys about Jesus, who is "of all our secrets the most telling and the most precious we have to tell."

Jesus once said, "Come to me, all of you who are weary and carry heavy burdens, and I will give you rest. Take my yoke upon you. Let me teach you, because I am humble and gentle, and you will find rest for your souls" (Matthew 11:28-29, NLT).

Who knows what burdens we carry inside of us? Some that we have picked up in our childhood, others in our adolescence, still others in our adult years. Who knows how heavy they have been to carry, or how long we have carried them, or how carrying them for so long has shaped us, stooped us, wearied us? Because of these burdens, a part of us is always weary, looking for a place to lay them down, some companionable place where we can find rest for our souls.

The closest I have come to experiencing rest for my soul in a book has been in those by Frederick Buechner. Through his writing, I have seen something of Christ.

Like Christ, he enfleshes words in such a way that they reach people where they live.

Like Christ, his voice is full of grace and truth.

Like Christ, he has resisted the temptation to defect from his calling, regardless how stark the wilderness or how seductive the food that was offered him there.

Like Christ, he has not been afraid to touch subjects that are shunned by others.

Like Christ, he speaks the words that in some way raise what is dead in all of us, heal what is sick, calm what is storming.

And like Christ, he gives rest to the weary.

Why, I've wondered, *do I feel so restful in the presence of his prose?* Honesty has a lot to do with it, I think.

There is a great line in the *thirtysomething* episode titled "Michael Writes a Story," when the unemployed advertising executive decides to enroll in an evening course on writing. The professor begins the first class with a short lecture on the craft of writing. "There are no rules in fiction," she says, "except honesty."

When I think of a characteristic that most captures the fiction of Frederick Buechner, as well as his nonfiction, *honesty* is the word that comes to mind. When I think about honesty, the story of Diogenes comes to mind.

109

Diogenes was a fourth-century Greek philosopher, who was regarded as a cynic—and for good reason, as the story illustrates. He is said to have traveled from town to town with a lantern in his hand, stopping people on the street, one after another, and shining the light in their face. He said nothing, just raised the lantern and stared into their eyes. When asked what he was doing, his reply was always the same: "I'm looking for an honest man."

Then, he lowered the lantern and walked away.

If Diogenes were to come to your town, your church, perhaps, and raise his lantern, what would he see, what would he say?

There are stories we don't tell in church. Secrets we don't share. Scars we don't reveal. Why? Often it's because those stories and secrets and scars aren't safe, either for those who tell them or for those who hear them. We take a risk in being honest about our lives.

People might distance themselves from us, gossip about us, try to fix us, keep a mental file on us, use what we say against us someday. Visitors at the church might get the wrong impression. Members might complain. Elders might keep an eye on us. It's a risk, a big risk— which is partly why we don't take the chance.

Sometimes it's easier to take a risk on paper rather than in person, putting it in the form of a book. For the last thirty or so years of my life, I have read a small library of books written by Christians, and my hope has always been to find an honest writer among them. It discourages me that too many times I have ended up lowering my lantern and walking away.

It's not my nature to be cynical. Sometimes, though, it's hard not to be. My reading habits, consequently, have changed. I no longer read topics of interest so much as I read writers who are honest, writers who tell the truth about their lives, especially about their lives with God.

I get suspicious of writers who have a reputation or a denomination to defend, an image to uphold or an ideology. C. S. Lewis once wrote that a doctrine never looked so threadbare as the one he had just successfully defended. One can defend a fortress, he explained, but not a landscape. When we reduce our faith to arguments, it becomes a fortress of manageable and therefore defensible size. But our faith is not a fortress. It is a sprawling landscape of rolling hills and pathless woods, rutted with steep and sometimes shadowy ravines. There are shimmering moments of wonder. There are also terrifying moments of wandering lost in the dark woods of our most looming, moss-covered fears.

What Frederick Buechner has been brave enough as a writer to do is to invite us to walk with him along the uneven and sometimes treacherous terrain of his own spiritual journey.

Artists work hard at discovering the core of things, the very center, regardless of how dangerous the journey or how daunting what they find there. Part of that journey is a spelunking trek into the deepest regions of the soul. The human soul, in general. Their own soul, in particular.

Who knows what is hidden away in those subterranean regions? Who knows what strange, sightless creatures slither around in there? Who knows what walls may collapse on us? Or what noxious gases may overwhelm us?

A Russian writer, whose name escapes me now, once said: "I don't know the heart of an evil man, but I know the heart of a good man . . . and it's bad."

It's a scary place to go alone. It's scarier still to take others along, give them a lantern, and let them take a look around. I think it was Emerson who said there is no fear like the fear of being known. The fear that when others see what is down there, they'll run off, shrieking. Or else they will see that there's nothing much down there at all, except an empty cavern with a few interesting rock formations, and they will leave disappointed at the fraudulent tourist attraction that is our lives.

Writing is a way of revealing who we are. It is also a way of hiding. In many ways, I have hidden behind my writing, especially at the start of my career. I wrote about other people, mostly, whether those people were in the Bible or in a novel or in real life. I grew up a fairly shy, self-conscious redheaded boy who didn't like attention. The boy followed me into adulthood, and although for much of the time I was able to keep him hidden, he was always standing off to the side, toeing the ground in my personal encounters as well as my creative endeavors.

When an editor asked me to consider writing something about my life as a creative person and how I nurtured it, I cringed.

My first response: "Why?"

To which she responded: "We think there's a market for a book like this."

"But why *me?*"

"We thought you would be a good person to speak to the subject."

"Who would read it? Besides a few family members, I don't know anyone else who would be even remotely interested in my life."

"Will you at least think about it?" she asked.

For a month, I did. After that time I gave her my answer. Which was yes. I came to the conclusion somewhat reluctantly (read: with a grocery sack over my head), thinking that it would be a good exercise for me to retrace the steps of my spiritual journey so I could gain a better understanding of where I had been and what had happened to me along the way.

The writing was awkward at first, and I felt self-conscious about it, the way you do the first time you take a shower in seventh grade after football practice and you realize there are no shower stalls. Just one, big, communal shower. Suddenly, you're faced with a choice. You can go home without taking a shower, of course, but if you do that every day, word will get around that you're a mama's boy. But if you take a shower with everybody else, they'll see you in your skinniness and your nakedness, and then who knows what words will make the rounds?

I finally finished the book, which was *Windows of the Soul.* What gave me the courage to write about my life was the way Frederick Buechner had written about his. He had written honestly and vulnerably, and in reading him, I felt a great burden lifted—that I was not alone.

"The story of any one of us," he wrote in *The Sacred Journey,* "is in some measure the story of us all." I learned the truth of that when I wrote about my own sacred journey. I couldn't have done it without someone like Frederick Buechner showing the way.

Driving home from visiting my mother in Texas, I got lost and somehow ended up in Archer City. It's a small town, stooped over with the weight of its years and the sketchy recollections of better times. Some of the storefronts around the town square were vacant, and from the looks of them, had been for years. I remembered Archer City from the Larry McMurtry book *The Last Picture Show.*

It was McMurtry's hometown, much the way he described it.

Except . . .

Except for a used bookstore, called Booked Up, that occupied not one, but several of the storefronts. I stopped, a little surprised at this stroke of good luck. I went in somewhat skeptically and browsed around. On the wall, I noticed a photograph of the actors in the film version of McMurtry's book. Then, in my curiosity, I opened a door that led to an expansive warehouse in the back, full of books. Must have been an acre of books, maybe more. All sorts of books. New ones. Old ones. One-of-a-kinds. And they had been sorted. By genre. By subject. Even by author. I couldn't believe it.

I felt like Kevin Costner's father in the final scene of *Field of Dreams,* where he looks around at the ball field with his eyes full of wonder, except it would be me asking the question, "Is this heaven?" To which the store clerk would reply, "No. It's Archer City."

I later asked the clerk how such an enormous bookstore happened to be located in such a small town. He told me it was owned by Larry McMurtry, who, as a hobby, bought up estates and bookstores that had gone out of business and shipped the books there.

I wondered if they had any Buechner books. Wandering the labyrinthine aisles, I found, to my surprise, an entire shelf of them.

I was excited.

Turning my head sideways and moving my hands slowly over the spines, I read the various titles, looking for ones I didn't have. I stopped at *Godric.* A work of fiction, based on a twelfth-century saint, it had been nominated for the Pulitzer Prize. I eased it from the shelf. It was in pristine condition. Opening the cover, I read the words: FIRST EDITION.

I was really excited.

Leafing through its pages, I came across a yellowed newspaper clipping, neatly folded. I gingerly unfolded it. My eyes went first to the black-and-white photograph of Buechner as a young man. Neatly groomed. White shirt. Dark coat and tie.

The clipping was a review of his book *A Long Day's Dying.* The opening paragraph read: "This first novel by a young man of 23 is a remarkable piece of work. There is a quality of civilized perception here, a sensitive and plastic handling of English prose and an ability to penetrate to the evanescent core of a human situation, all proclaiming major talent."

What a moment! There he was, a young man just out of college, his whole life lying open before him like the blank pages of a writer's journal . . . before he had married . . . before he had kids . . . before he had a career.

Okay, now I was *really, really* excited.

I started going through all of his books, fanning their pages, hoping to find something else. After doing this to about a dozen books, a letter fell to the floor. Picking it up, I read the return address. The name *Buechner* was scrawled in green ink.

Hands trembling, I opened the envelope to discover it was an inquiry he had sent to a rare-book store in New York, regarding the poet Edith Nesbit. He had circled the book he wanted, a signed, second edition they had in stock, with these words of explanation: "I'd very much like this one & enclose my check. Many thanks, F. Buechner."

It is hard to convey the thrill I felt just holding a letter of his in my hand. I respected him so much. And I had learned so much from him.

Several years later, an older cousin of mine, the Reverend Milton Gire, a Baptist pastor in the state of Washington, called to say he had read a book of mine and enjoyed it and just wanted to say hello. He was my father's brother's son, twenty-seven years my senior. I had met him once or twice in my childhood but had had no contact with him since then. He'd noticed I had quoted Buechner several times in my book, and he said he had read several of Buechner's books. In fact, he had corresponded with the author years earlier.

When Milton passed away in 1998, his wife sent me his obituary from the local newspaper, pictures of the two of them, and the bulletin from his funeral service. She sent them pressed inside the covers of *The Life of Jesus,* an out-of-print book by Buechner that Milton had known I didn't have.

Tucked in the pages were two letters. One was post-marked 1976. The other, 1977.

The second one was addressed:

The Rev. Milton L. Gire
First Baptist Church
105 W. 6th St.
Port Angeles, Washington 98362

The first one was addressed to:

The Rev. Miles
Baptist Church
Port Angeles, Washington

Interesting, I thought. I wonder why Milton had a letter addressed to a Rev. Miles? I opened it and read the handwritten note.

Dear Mr. Miles,
Do I remember your name right? Did you write me a particularly warm and generous letter about reading a book of mine Wishful Thinking? *—at a time when you were recovering from an illness? Will you overlook the dismal fuzzy-headedness that led me somehow to lose your letter so that I have nothing but an uncertain memory of your name and address?*

The letter went on to say how much he appreciated the words my cousin had written him and how timely an encouragement they were at that juncture in his life, particularly his life as a writer.

His words were characteristically honest. But what touched me even more than the honesty of the words was the humility of the gesture. Even though Buechner had lost my cousin's letter, he made an effort to reconstruct it in his mind and to recall as much as he could about his name and address.

How many people do you know who would have done that? It would have been so easy to dismiss it or to wait for a follow-up letter. After all, if it were important, he would write again, wouldn't he? But Buechner didn't dismiss it, didn't wait for another letter. He answered *this* one, the one he lost and only partially recalled.

How it got to my cousin, I'll never know. No zip code. No specific Baptist church named. And the last name was wrong. Somehow, though, it traveled more than three thousand miles to bless my cousin . . . and across twenty years to bless me.

Of all the things I've read of Buechner's, this to me is the most beautiful.

Who knows what my cousin needed at that juncture in his own life? Maybe he needed more than a book. Maybe he needed a letter. Maybe at some time or another we all need a letter, a letter that in some way has something of Jesus in it, reaching out to us across country, across time, to remind us . . . that we are not alone.

When I look back on this movement in the dance, the individual steps seem meanderingly unprovidential. The first Buechner book came to me serendipitously. The phone call from my cousin came out of the blue. I stumbled onto the bookstore in Archer City, where there happened to be a shelf of Buechner's books, where a yellowed newspaper clipping and an inconsequential letter happened to be pressed in the pages, sacraments of who he was, sacraments that few would have treasured as much as I did. My cousin's wife sent me a Buechner book I didn't have, along with two of his letters her husband had saved. Was it a dying request? *Send this to Ken when I'm gone. It will mean a lot to him.*

Tears come to my eyes as I retrace those steps. With the tears comes a sense of the sacredness of each and every step of the dance, even the spontaneous ones that at the time seem to be leading nowhere. Until we retrace them. Learning as we go. Looking beyond the randomness of our steps to the rhythms of his grace.

We are not alone, you and I, as much as it feels that way sometimes. And we are not lost, regardless of where the shuffling of our feet takes us. We are being led somewhere, whether it's to a big city or Archer City. And along the way, every step of the way, there is music playing in the background . . . if only we have ears to hear it and the heart to grasp its theme.

THE DISSONANCE
OF THE DANCE

What suspense and conflict are to the drama, dissonance is to music. It creates the areas of tension without which the areas of relaxation would have no meaning. Each complements the other; both are a necessary part of the artistic whole.

JOSEPH MACHLIS, *THE ENJOYMENT OF MUSIC*

The movie *The Jerk* is about a man, played by Steve Martin, who has grown up in a poor, black family. Martin always suspected he had been adopted, but he wasn't sure why he felt that way. It didn't occur to him that maybe it was because he was white as a porcelain sink. What did occur to him was that he was the only person in the family with no rhythm. Everyone else in the family danced so naturally, but he could never keep in step with them, his movements looking less like dancing and more like the first halting stages of a grand mal seizure.

When I imagine myself dancing, the picture that comes to mind isn't Fred Astaire in the movie *Top Hat*. It isn't Gene Kelly in *Singin' in the Rain*. It's Steve Martin in *The Jerk*.

Every summer for the past six years I have spoken at a Christian family camp in Estes Park, Colorado, called Wind River Ranch. One evening each week they bring in two professional square dancers to teach the guests the basic steps and turns of the dance. If there were such a category as "less-than-a-beginner," that would be mine.

Every time I try to square-dance, my feet get tangled. I always seem to be going right when I should be going left, always bumping into someone, always apologizing. I have to think so much about the steps and concentrate so hard on my feet that it hurts my brain. As a rhythmically challenged person, I not only don't dance well, I don't even clap well. During worship when people are clapping to a song, I have to single out someone and watch their hands to keep mine in sync with the music.

My sense of rhythm in the spiritual realm isn't a whole lot better. God knows I have put myself out there on the dance floor and tried my best to learn. But my feet always seem to get tangled. I always seem to be going right when I should be going left, always bumping into someone. Always apologizing. To God, mostly. But also to those close to me, to those whose toes I have stepped on, whose feet I have stumbled over, whose dance I have disrupted.

I'm better at dancing than I used to be, but it is still hard. I find I not only need the music to get me to dance, I need someone to lead me in the dance. I need a partner.

From the missteps in my spiritual life, I have learned a few things about dancing with Jesus. The most important is this: If we fall in love, our feet will follow. If we draw close to him and stay close, we won't have to worry about our feet or where he may be leading them.

That doesn't mean we won't step on his toes.

It doesn't mean we won't trip over our own feet.

It doesn't mean we won't bump into other people.

What it does mean is that Jesus will be with us through all the complicated steps and the sudden turns, steadying us if we stumble, picking us up if we fall, doing whatever it takes to keep us dancing.

Our greatest missteps occur during the dissonant parts of the dance. We stumble not so much when the rhythms are pleasant and predictable as when they become grating and erratic. Whenever there is dissonance in music or in drama or in dancing, it is because certain rhythms need to be broken in order for new rhythms to be established. This is important to understand. Dissonance is about transition, and therefore it is a necessary part of the artistic whole.

125

I'm not referring here to moral dissonance, which has to do with taking steps that are ethically wayward. I'm referring to other forms of dissonance that serve as transitions in our lives—vocational ones, financial ones, relational ones, as well as theological ones.

As a writer, I work hard at transitions. I try to make them smooth so the reader can be taken from one idea to another without feeling the jolt of movement. Life, however, is not a book, and life transitions are seldom smooth. Sometimes they are jarring. Occasionally, even devastating.

As I look back on it, the process of becoming a writer feels very much like a dance I was drawn into. Not unlike the "Emperor Waltz," the first steps were light and easy to follow. The rhythms were pleasant and enjoyable. I felt honored by the call to write. I felt ennobled by the specific movement in the dance when I finished my first book.

Then came the dissonant part.

As I made the transition to becoming a writer, the rhythms of my life, once so pleasant and predictable, began to break down. The book didn't sell—and nothing else did either. The money I had invested in my career ran out. The steps got harder. My feet got clumsier. And what had once seemed an exhilarating dance now felt more like the trudging cadence of a death march.

What was happening? New rhythms were being introduced into my life while I was trying to hold on to the old ones. I wanted to go new places on the dance floor but keep the old rhythms, the rhythms I knew, the rhythms I felt comfortable with, the rhythms I could dance to.

Along the way in my vocation, Jesus spoke, not only introducing new rhythms into the dance but revealing the next step. While I was working on my master's thesis, for example, he spoke to me through the joy I had in writing it. As a student, I wasn't stirred by theological books. I didn't like taking dictation in class or studying for tests. But I loved writing papers. And of them all, I loved writing my master's thesis the most.

While I was working on my first book, *Treasure in an Oatmeal Box,* Jesus spoke to me not through my joy but through my tears. The story was about a year in the life of a set of ten-year-old twins, one of whom was mentally handicapped. In the course of writing the

126

story, I developed a deep affection for this fictional character I had created, so much so, that when it came to the next-to-last chapter where he would die, I couldn't write it. I had to write the last chapter first, then I went back to write the other one. I cried all the way through the pages of those chapters. I had never done that in a sermon I had prepared or in a class I had taught. But I had done it here, and I believe it was the Lord's way of leading me into what he wanted me to do with my life.

From there the Lord led me to California, not to USC, where I had hoped to get training as a writer, but to Insight for Living, where I actually got a job as a writer. The job taught me how to edit, a task at which I had no skill. While there, I worked evenings and weekends on my own writing. Book after book not only got finished but got published, and that is how my career as a writer began.

I tried during this time to listen well. I had not been a particularly good listener in the past, and this was one of the new rhythms the Lord was introducing into my life. One routine day at work, I thought I heard him whispering through a moment in the Scriptures, the moment where Mary anoints Jesus with costly perfume. I wasn't sure at first that it was Jesus speaking, and if it was, I wasn't sure what he was saying. After weeks of straining to hear, I gradually came to the realization that he was inviting me to partner with him on a series of devotional books that began with *Intimate Moments with the Savior*. It took me awhile to follow him into that movement of the dance, but with each step I took, I fell a little more in love with him. And that, I believe, more than anything else, was the purpose of that part of the dance.

Other projects to which the Lord led me were *Windows of the Soul* and *The Weathering Grace of God.* An editor suggested one, a publisher the other. And though I resisted the one and hesitated with the other, looking back, I believe it was his voice speaking to me through theirs.

As I look back on it, that time was a Babel of voices. Inner voices mostly—the voice of ego, the voice of anxiety, the voice of expediency, the voice of desperation. But also the voices of others. The hopeful voices of editors, suggesting projects. The practical voices of publishers, rejecting projects. The sometimes clamoring voices of other people with stories of their own that they felt convinced God wanted me to tell, either with them or for them.

What quieted the cacophony of those voices was the clarity of Christ's voice.

But I had to draw near to hear it. I had to listen well, and sometimes long. At all times, though, I had to prepare my heart to make room for those "manger moments" when divine words were swaddled in the lowliest and sometimes unlikeliest of ways.

Although I heard the Lord speak in a number of different ways regarding my writing, I heard him speak specifically only once. It happened one night when I was at a friend's house. The phone rang. It was my wife. She told me she had just heard on the news that a friend of ours, Dave Dravecky, was going to have his arm amputated. Her voice cracked as she said it. After hanging up, I fought the emotion, told my friend I needed to go, then drove home.

I had met Dave less than two years earlier when his book *Comeback* was published. We had the same literary agent at the time, and that is how we met. Dave was a pitcher for the San Francisco Giants when a malignant tumor in his pitching arm ended his career. Told he would not have much use of his arm after the surgery, Dave believed he would not only regain full mobility but he would even pitch again, and in the major leagues. He had a lot of faith, a lot of courage, a lot of determination. He worked hard, and as the story unfolded, he did come back to pitch again. But then the story took a tragic turn. His arm, brittle from all the radiation treatments, broke one day while he was pitching in Montreal. The resultant surgery was complicated, and the doctor told him if it wasn't successful, he might lose his arm. I had hoped and prayed it would never come to that, but that night it had.

129

It was raining as I was driving. With the rain fell a steady stream of emotions. And with the emotions, an intermittent pelting of thoughts. The *tick-swoosh* of the windshield wipers swept each thought away as quickly as it splashed in my mind.

"Oh, God." *Tick-swoosh.*

"What should I do?" *Tick-swoosh.*

"Should I call, send a letter?" *Tick-swoosh.*

"Send a ham, maybe?" *Tick-swoosh.*

That's when I clearly heard: "You can write his story."

Tick-swoosh. Tick-swoosh. Tick-swoosh.

"What story would that be?" *Tick-swoosh.*

"What do you do when you can't come back?" *Tick-swoosh.*

Even though the voice was clear, I was unsure of myself, feeling a little insecure about my ability to hear God's voice, a little pretentious about suggesting a book on somebody else's life, and a little self-serving about offering to write it.

Some kind of confirmation would help. The next evening, I was flipping through the television channels and paused on the movie *Field of Dreams*. I love that movie, but I had seen it two or three times before. I was getting ready to change channels when something Shoeless Joe Jackson said caught my attention. It was the scene where he was talking about how it felt to be ejected so suddenly and so finally from the game he so dearly loved. "It was like having a part of me amputated," he said. That word, especially in that context, felt like the confirmation I was looking for. Still I wasn't sure. As I watched the movie, the themes of the book started coming together.

Even then, I wasn't definitely sure. But I was definitely getting surer.

The next morning, I called my agent. I explained what I had heard in the car and on the television, and I asked him what he thought. I'm not sure what he thought about the voice, but he loved the idea. I asked him to call Dave, and if Dave felt that this was the story God wanted to tell through his life, then I would be honored to write it.

Dave felt sure it was. And finally I felt sure, too.

The book was titled *When You Can't Come Back,* and it includes three scenes from *Field of Dreams* that jumped out at me that night at my house.

Before this idea came to me, the publisher had already discussed the possibility of a second book with Dave and his agent. And the two of them had already talked with me about writing it. But I had mixed feelings about the book they suggested. One reason was that there were a lot of books that had already been written on the subject they were proposing, and I didn't think that I, as a writer, had much, if anything, to contribute.

I was asked to pray about it. I said I would. I lied.

The publishing company had editorial meetings to bat around other ideas. One of the editors pitched me one of those ideas to see if I would be interested. I wasn't. Conceptually, the idea had merit; I just had no passion for it. Part of the reason I had no passion for it was that it felt less like a story God was wanting told and more like just good marketing strategy. I explained my feelings to the editor. I also explained that I didn't want to exploit my relationship with Dave by having the possibility of a book deal as a hidden agenda. I thought that was the end of all the conversations about the book.

And it was, at least for me. Until another voice entered the conversation. In truth, I think that voice had been speaking all along. To Dave. To his agent. To the publisher. To the editor. And to me.

Why I heard it then so clearly, I don't know.

Why I don't hear it that clearly more often, I don't know either.

If I did hear his voice more clearly more often, it would make the dance a lot easier, I know that. Especially the dissonant parts.

Perhaps one of the reasons we don't hear Christ's voice more clearly is that he wants to draw us into such a close embrace that the slightest move of his hand against the small of our back tells us all we need to know.

With couples who have danced together for a long time, there is an intuitive language that passes between them, a language so sublime it sometimes renders words unnecessary.

The first time I played the "Emperor Waltz" publicly, it was to an audience of more than three thousand. Everyone on the program that day was allotted a lean portion of time, trimmed to the second. I knew that before I came, so I was a little self-conscious (read: chewing my nails down to the quick) about my part. For the morning devotional, I was allotted thirty minutes. The "Emperor Waltz" takes twelve. I thought about editing it down. Partly for myself, because that left me only eighteen minutes to develop my thoughts. Partly also for the audience, because twelve minutes is a long time to sit with your eyes closed and imagine yourself dancing. I thought if I could edit the dance down to six minutes, it might not be such a stretch. There were a number of places in the dance that were repetitive, and if I could cut some of those, I reasoned, it would help. My first choice, though, was to cut the one dissonant part. It confused me why it was in there. It didn't seem to belong—and besides, I didn't like it.

As I thought about editing the dance, I realized something. Although the shorter version would be easier for my audience to sit through, in making it easier I would be undermining the very point I was trying to make: It is *his* dance, not ours. And if that is true of the dance as a whole, it is true of the individual movements within the dance, however repetitive they are, or however dissonant. Since it isn't our dance, we not only don't have the right to edit it, we don't have the power to edit it.

133

Sometimes I forget that. And sometimes I forget this, as well: We have been invited to dance, not to choreograph.

Still, the more dissonant the dance, the harder it is to believe that there is any choreographer behind the steps, let alone a divine one. It seems the steps are a mistake and that the best thing to do is to get through that part as quickly as we can. Perhaps longer strides or faster footwork are what we need.

That's seldom the case.

Then what *do* we need? When the room starts to spin and it feels as if we are falling away, what do we do? How do we get through those parts? We get through them the same way Jesus got through them. How dizzy he must have felt the night of his betrayal when he was caught in the spin of those circumstances. What did he do to get through it? He drew closer, and he held on tighter. He got alone with his Father, threw himself at his feet, begging to sit out the steps that lay ahead, but finally surrendering to the dissonant rhythms the Father was leading him through, however difficult they were to follow.

Drawing closer, holding on tighter.

That is what Gethsemane was all about.

That is what the upper room was about. Jesus drawing the disciples closer and embracing them tighter than ever before. Even so, they all fell away (see Mark 14:27). Even the one most determined not to (see verses 29-31). After his resurrection, Jesus returned to them as he had promised (see verse 28). At one time or another he returned to all of them (see 1 Corinthians 15:5). He returned to the two despondent disciples on the road to Emmaus (see Luke 24). To his brother James (see 1 Corinthians 15:7). To Peter and others (see John 21:1-17).

Why did he return? He returned to restore some of the old rhythms that had broken down in the transition, but also to introduce them to some of the new rhythms he would be leading them in (see Acts 1:1-8).

I still love you, he seems to be saying to Peter when he returned to him. I still love you, even though you fell away, even though you stumbled, even though you stepped on my toes. I still love you, and I still want to dance with you.

There is a delightful song someone sent me earlier this year by an Australian woman named Robby. The song is titled "You Can Dance on My Toes." The refrain goes like this:

And I want you to know
That I'm so much in love with you
And I don't really mind if
You dance on my toes

The lyrics I think express the heart of Christ. I think
he so much wants us to dance with him that he doesn't
mind if we step on his toes in the process. I don't think
he wants us looking at our feet, worrying about whether
we are going to step on his toes or he is going to step
on ours. It's going to happen, especially during the
dissonant parts of the dance. It's going to happen, and
it's going to be okay. If love covers a multitude of sins,
certainly it covers a few missteps on the dance floor.

135

THE TEMPTATION
OF THE DANCE

Martha Graham and her fellow dance pioneers were ready to discard all the old rules. They wanted to create a new kind of dance, a uniquely American dance that would capture the spirit and energy of their country and their times.

RUSSELL FREEDMAN, *MARTHA GRAHAM: A DANCER'S LIFE*

S he died at her home on April 1, 1991. Her death made headlines around the world. The front page of the *New York Times* read: MARTHA GRAHAM DIES AT 96: A REVOLUTIONARY IN DANCE.

Hailed as the mother of modern dance, Graham achieved her goal of creating a new kind of dance that was uniquely American. Courageous, independent, and visionary, she was a completely original artist, often compared to Picasso and Stravinsky. A legendary dancer who performed all over the world, she was an even more legendary choreographer, creating more than two hundred original dances, many of them enduring works of art. In doing so, she gave the world an entirely new vocabulary within the language of dance, allowing dancers to express themselves in new and innovative ways.

Graham dedicated herself completely to her art, sacrificing everything. She was driven not only by her passion but also by her perfectionism. Night after grueling night, she practiced, often alone, "trying," as she put it, "to find strange, beautiful movements of my own."

A tireless worker, she continued working until the day she died, putting the finishing touches on a new dance she called *The Eyes of the Goddess,* a work commissioned by Spain to commemorate the five hundredth anniversary of the voyage of Columbus to America.

Martha Graham's entire life was driven by self-expression. It made her a legend in the dance world. And for dancers all over the world, it made her a role model. In the spiritual world, however, her life is more cautionary than exemplary.

As a creative person, it is humbling to acknowledge this, but the Scriptures place little value on our need to express ourselves in unique and original ways. Our life with Christ is a dance, but it is not a dance we create. Our work is not about trying to find movements that are uniquely our own and finding innovative ways to express them. It's about trying to find movements that are uniquely *his* own and simply following them.

There are innovators in Christian ministry who are as dedicated as Martha Graham, equally driven, and equally gifted in creating new kinds of dances. Innovative people, though, are particularly susceptible to the seduction of the self. The temptation is as old as Eden and as beguiling as forbidden fruit. At the core of the temptation is the deception that what matters more than anything else in life is expressing *our* ideas, achieving *our* goals, actualizing *our* dreams.

The dance we have been invited to participate in is not about the realization of the self but rather the relinquishment of the self. Surrendering himself is the way

Jesus lived his life, from the day of his birth to the day of his death. Each and every day he was faced with the temptations to live for himself—to defend himself, advance himself, exalt himself. Yet each and every day he resisted them.

When approached on one of those days by Satan himself, Jesus resisted each of his temptations. The temptation to take his life into his own hands, to make things happen in his own time and his own way (see Matthew 4:3). The temptation to be associated with the spectacular, attracting not only attention but acclaim (see verses 5-6). The temptation to acquire kingdoms, along with the power and glory that went with them (see verses 8-9).

When others approached Jesus with similar temptations, he responded the same way. Exalt yourself, said those who wanted to make him king. And though he was destined for a throne, he resisted the temptation to ascend a throne that had been prepared for him by human hands. Defend yourself, said Pilate when Jesus stood before him. And though legions of angels were at his disposal, he resisted the temptation to do so. Save yourself, said those who watched him die. And though with a word he could have, he resisted the temptation, choosing to save others instead.

The life of our Lord could be summed up in a sentence. "The Son of Man did not come to be served, but to serve, and to give His life a ransom for many" (Matthew 20:28). His life wasn't about expressing himself. Or enriching himself. Or exalting himself.

It was about emptying himself.

In trying to come up with an illustration of the way Jesus lived his life, a book comes to mind. And with the book, a person.

The book is *The Giving Tree* by Shel Silverstein. It is a children's book, or so it seems by the cover. The cover is lime green with a darker green tree to the right that is extending a red apple from one of its leafy branches to the outstretched arms of a barefoot boy in a green T-shirt and a pair of short, red coveralls. It is an endearing cover.

Until you turn the book over.

On the back is a full-page, black-and-white photo of the author, a grizzly bear of a man with a bald head and dark piercing eyes, flared nostrils, a full beard, and teeth bared as if he were about to say something like what Robert DeNiro said in the movie *Taxi Driver:* "You talkin' to me? . . . You there, little kid with the book in your hands, you talkin' to *me?*" Or something Clint Eastwood might say with a curled lip in one of his Dirty Harry movies: "Go ahead, punk, read it. Make my day."

The story is only 624 words long, with simple ink drawings by the author; and despite the gruff-looking photograph on the back cover, it couldn't be a more tender story.

It begins: "Once there was a tree . . . and she loved a little boy."

The story is about their relationship over the course of the little boy's life, chronicling his childhood, adolescence, adulthood, middle age, and old age.

In his youth, the little boy gathers the tree's leaves and makes them into crowns, pretending to be king of the forest. He playfully climbs her trunk, swings from her branches, eats her apples, sleeps in her shade.

"And the boy loved the tree," the author comments.

"And the tree was happy."

As the boy grows into adolescence, he spends less and less time with the tree, preferring instead the company of a young woman. One day the boy comes back, needing money. The tree has no money to give, but she tells the boy to gather her apples so he can sell them and get the money he needs.

143

The boy stays away a long time, which makes the tree sad.

One day the boy returns as an adult. He wants to get married and raise a family, he tells the tree. But he needs a house to do that, so he asks the tree for a house. The tree tells the boy he can take her branches and use them to build a house. When he leaves, the tree is bare.

Later in his manhood, the boy returns again. He is older now and seems disappointed with life. He asks the tree for a boat so he can sail far away. The tree offers to let him cut down her trunk so he can make a boat and sail away and be happy. There is now nothing left of the tree but a stump.

When the boy is old and shriveled, he returns to the tree one last time. The conversation goes like this:

"I am sorry, Boy," said the tree, "but I have nothing left to give you—My apples are gone."

"My teeth are too weak for apples," said the boy.

"My branches are gone," said the tree. "You cannot swing on them—"

"I am too old to swing on branches," said the boy.

"My trunk is gone," said the tree. "You cannot climb—"

"I am too tired to climb," said the boy.

"I am sorry that I could not give you something . . . but I have nothing left. I am just an old stump."

The boy tells the tree that he is tired, and that all he needs is a quiet place to sit and rest. Elated that she still has something to give, however small a gift, she invites the boy to sit and rest.

The next page is a drawing of the tired old man sitting on the stump, with these words: "And the boy did."

The next page is empty, except for these words: "And the tree was happy."

The book ends there, creating a moment of rest, not just for the boy but also for the reader. In that restful moment is time to reflect. "Once there was a tree . . . and she loved a little boy." The happiness of the tree was in giving herself to the boy she loved, giving all of herself for all of the boy's life. It is a poignant story about life, about relationships, about love, about growing up and growing old.

I grew up amid an orchard of "giving trees," people who freely and generously gave of their lives. Some were family members. Others were friends. Some were only acquaintances—and a few were complete strangers. They gave me branches to play in, shade to rest in, apples to be nourished by, wood to build with, stumps to sit on.

And it made them happy.

That was their beauty.

Of all the giving trees in my life, none gave more freely or more generously than my mother. Having watched my wife give birth to our four children, I am amazed at all that a mother gives just to bring another life into the world, let alone what it takes to nourish and care for that life.

My mother tells me I was an easy birth. I came quickly and without much pain. Even so, there were still the 2 A.M. feedings, dirty diapers, and soiled clothes. Later, there were all the childhood diseases—from measles to pneumonia—and all the childhood traumas—from stitches on the head to a broken leg.

The broken leg happened when I was four—on Christmas Eve. Even at that early age, I knew that all sorts of surprises lay hidden around the house. Spying some candy on a shelf in a storage cabinet, I started my climb. On the second or third shelf, I slipped, and when I instinctively grabbed the cabinet, it fell on me, breaking my leg near the hip.

Because I was so young, the doctor feared that if he put a cast only on the broken leg, the other leg would grow longer. Instead, he gave me a full body cast, which started just below my shoulders and covered both of my legs. For several months I couldn't walk—couldn't hardly move.

I don't remember the pain nearly as much as the itching, which I couldn't scratch because of the cast. Day after day, Mom would take a straightened coat hanger and scratch my illusive itches. She brought my meals, played with me, read me books, emptied my bedpans, washed the little bit of me that showed, and did who knows how many hundreds of other things during the course of my recovery.

My brother had just been born that September, so Mom had a newborn to take care of, along with her other domestic responsibilities. Each morning, she had to get my sister ready for school. She had clothes to wash and iron. Housework. The evening meal. Dishes. A husband who . . . well, if you're a woman and you have one, you know all that entails.

When Dad had a near-fatal heart attack at thirty-nine, Mom went to work. Over the years, Dad had two open-heart surgeries and contracted hepatitis from a blood transfusion, which put him out of work for an entire year. For more than ten years, Mom worked to help with the hospital bills and with the needs of a growing family.

She got up every morning around 4:30, made all of us sack lunches for school, made breakfast for everyone, then left for work. She came home around 4:30 or so in the afternoon, made dinner, got all of our clothes ready for the next day, then went to bed so she could wake up to do it all over again the next day. On the weekends, she cleaned house, washed clothes, went grocery shopping. I don't know how she did it all.

I asked her for a lot, or so it seems to me now.

"Will you iron this shirt for tonight?"

"Could you wash my basketball uniform for tomor-row?"

"I need my report typed by Monday. Would you mind doing it?"

I never remember her saying no, not to things like that anyway, not when it came to giving of her time. I don't remember asking her much for money, but I don't remember her ever saying no, if she had it to give. She spent precious little of her time or her money on herself, that much I do remember.

Dad died seventeen years ago, in 1986. Last year, Mom turned eighty. She's had three strokes, from which she has recovered remarkably well. A few years ago, she broke a vertebra in her back and ever since has been frail and tentative. Mentally, though, she is still sharp. She reads everything I send her and puts in a little time each day on her crossword puzzles. She was always good with words, always had a good vocabulary. If we ever needed to know how a word was spelled, we never went to the dictionary; we went to her. Her hearing is bad, so I have to raise my voice to talk with her, which tends to keep the conversations short and not very involved.

147

But she has other conversations, some of which are quite long and often very involved. Those are the conversations she has with God. She prays faithfully and fervently for all her children and grandchildren. "I can't do much else," she explains, almost apologetically. With so many of her branches gone, along with her leaves and her fruit, it is what she has left to give. She gives it freely and generously and, more importantly, joyfully.

That is her beauty.

Once there was a mom . . . and she loved a little boy.

When Jesus said he came not to be served but to serve, and to give his life a ransom for many, the little boy understood. He understood from the shade his mother had given him—from the fruit, the branches, and everything else she had sacrificed over the years, down to the very stump.

And the boy loved the tree.

And the tree was happy.

That was her life. Those were her steps. Unlike Martha Graham, her dance was neither unique nor innovative nor expressive. She is not the mother of modern dance. But she is *my* mother. And, in my opinion, a better dancer.

THE FEAR
OF THE DANCE

Oh, the places you'll go.

DR. SEUSS, *OH, THE PLACES YOU'LL GO!*

The fear of the dance is the fear of where Christ may lead us and what he may ask of us once we get there. The place we fear may be seminary or South America. It may be married with children or single and celibate. It may be poverty. Or great responsibility. Or suffering. Or public speaking.

Fear is something I have struggled with in one form or another most of my life. As a child, I was afraid of a lot of things. Some of those things were snakes and spankings and shadows lurking in the closet, which I suppose all children fear. Not all that many kids, though, are afraid of the Second Coming, which was one of the things that scared me, with all the hushed talk of the end of the world, everything in flames and all sorts of things falling from the sky, earthquakes and famines, wars and rumors of wars, persecution. I remember as a child overhearing a verse that said that no one knows the day or the hour of Christ's return, and as only a child would reason, I woke up every morning after that, saying out loud and with great conviction that this was the day Christ was going to come back. The logic, of course, was that it couldn't be *that* day because a kid at 5709 South Schilder Drive knew it, and if Christ did return that day, it would make God a liar, which I felt reasonably certain he would not allow to happen.

Most of my fears as a young Christian centered around places I feared God would send me. I felt safe slouched in the corner of a distant pew, but I had an ominous feeling that if I sat too close to the front God would call on me for something, kind of the way teachers called on their favorite students in the front rows. I didn't mind washing blackboards or running errands, but I figured that if God were the one doing the calling, he would be expecting great and heroic things of me, things I wasn't sure I was up to. He might even ask me to be a martyr, like the ones I heard about in Sunday school, and I was sure I wasn't up to that.

In my book *Windows of the Soul,* I recount some of those fears. "I feared that God would call me to the place I least wanted to go. Africa. And that he would call me to the work I least wanted to do. Missionary work. Hacking through a jungle with a machete, swatting at mosquitoes in the sweltering heat, dodging poison darts. I remembered the Tarzan movies. I remembered them better than the Sunday school stories. 'Bwana, look out! Simba!' I remembered the lions and the alligators and the boa constrictors that squeezed the life from your body and swallowed you whole. And did you see the episode with the quicksand? Anywhere, God. Anywhere but Africa."

Yet in so many turns of the dance that Christ has

been leading me in, Africa has brushed by me. Is there
a pattern to those steps, I wonder? Or am I imposing
a pattern on them? I'm not sure. But I am sure he
would want me to consider those steps, to reflect on
them, to discover where they may be leading and what
he is offering me there, or asking of me.

The first step happened serendipitously, or so it
seemed then, a number of years ago when I lived in
Fullerton, California. One evening I drove across town
so my eldest daughter could attend a Bible study at
someone's house in the city of Orange. It was such a
slow drive through the snarl of southern California traf-
fic that I didn't want to go home just to have to turn
right around and drive back. Instead, I drove around
the neighborhood after I dropped my daughter off,
looking for some companionable place to pass the next
couple of hours.

In my meanderings, I happened upon Chapman
College. I parked my car and went into the Thurmond
Clarke Memorial Library. The library was cool and
quiet, and as I passed through its doors, I felt an unseen
presence almost hushing me. Immediately I noticed a
collection of photographs and mementos, donated to
the college by Lee and Dorothy Ellerbrock, a husband
and wife team who had served with Albert Schweitzer
from 1953 to 1965 at his hospital in Lambaréné, Africa.

A series of black-and-white photographs loomed
from the walls on thick poster board, showing the
doctor in a variety of settings. His features were unfor-
gettable. He had a full shock of white hair, looking as if
it had been swept back once in the early morning by a

153

hasty hand and for the rest of the day lay forgotten. His eyes were dark and sunken, with tired bags sagging beneath them. His nose was large. His face, weathered.

Various memorabilia were displayed in glass cases. A coarsely woven, white linen shirt with broad pockets. A pair of gold-rimmed spectacles. A fountain pen. Handwritten notebooks, their pages slightly warped from the jungle humidity. Several letters he had written to the countless people who had corresponded with him over the years. He had published books on theology, philosophy, music, and medicine, some of which were also on display. A map of Africa showed the location, in what is now the Republic of Gabon, where Schweitzer started his hospital in 1913. Several photographs showed the people of Gabon, as well as Gabonese fabric and artifacts.

A number of signposts during his early life had pointed Schweitzer toward Africa. One was the parable of the rich man and Lazarus. After reflecting on it, he felt that the rich man was Europe and Africa was Lazarus. How could he enjoy the abundance of his own country, he reasoned, when his African neighbors lived in such misery?

A driven student, Schweitzer earned doctorates in philosophy, music, and theology. Upon finishing a fourth doctorate in 1938, this time in medicine, he spent the remaining fifty-two years of his life relieving the suffering of the natives who lived within a two-hundred-mile radius of the obscure, jungle hospital he built in French Equatorial Africa.

He went to Africa under the auspices of the conservative Missionary Society of Paris, but because of his theological views he agreed not to preach there but only to practice medicine. Years later, he told journalist Norman Cousins: "I decided to make my life my argument. I would advocate the things I believed in terms of the life I lived and what I did."

When I left the library, something of Schweitzer went with me. I found myself picking up several books about him, along with a few books by him. I found, quite by accident, some recordings of him performing Bach on the organ. He was at the time the world's foremost authority on the composer and toured Europe playing his works.

So many of Schweitzer's words have moved me, but it is the words of those who knew him that have moved me the most. In her book *Albert Schweitzer's Gift of Friendship,* Erica Anderson, who had sustained a friendship with the doctor through thirty-five years of correspondence, wrote a touching story of something that happened on Schweitzer's seventy-eighth birthday. For several days before the birthday, people had been quietly preparing for it. Children had gathered mangoes for him. One of the nurses had carved some funny looking animals out of wood. Another nurse had painted a jungle landscape, which she had everyone sign. Erica Anderson had taken a photograph of Schweitzer's favorite wild pig to present to him.

On the morning of his birthday, natives and staff members gathered in the dining room to surprise him. The tables had been decorated with garlands of leaves and flowers from the jungle. As he entered, everyone

began to sing. After coffee, he opened the gifts and
thanked each person individually. When breakfast was
over, a choir of young native voices sang outside the
dining room. Schweitzer went outside to hear them,
his head bowed as he listened.

As they were finishing their song, a latecomer arrived
with his present. The man was a native who Schweitzer
had treated for leprosy years earlier. He was old and
thin and his hands were maimed. He spoke to the group
gathered outside, telling them that he had a present
consisting of a few words, and he would like everyone
there to hear it. Facing Schweitzer, he told him:

> Grand Docteur, today I want to thank you and tell
> everybody how you have helped me. I am only one
> among many. One cannot count them, so give me
> your ear and listen to what I have to say. It was in
> 1913 that we learned that you would come to us,
> to care for us as a doctor. I, Ephé, was still quite
> a young man then. I'd prepared myself to become
> a preacher. Since 1910 I'd known that I was a leper.
> It was that year that I first saw the spots, red ones,
> on my body. That made me very sad. I came to you
> and you gave yourself great pain with me. You gave
> me the oil of chaulmoogra and it helped me. There
> was a great improvement in my disease, not only
> because of the oil, but because you shared with me
> my sorrow. You treated me like your sick brother,
> and my heart was made much lighter. I walked
> from village to village and preached, and I told the
> listeners that the Grand Docteur was our brother,

who had come to stay with us to help us against the
terrible disease to which we fall prey. But in later
years, when the war took you away from us, my
illness became worse again. I often thought of you
and thought wonderingly whether God would send
you back to us. I prayed for it, for your return,
Grand Docteur, but my illness became worse and
worse. My hands became deformed. I lost weight.
I had the fever and great sores opened up on my feet.
One day when I had almost lost hope, I heard you
had come back. I begged my brothers to carry me to
you. "Ephé," you said. "Ephé, my friend, here I am
to help you again."

You built for me a hut for myself because no one
else could share my place with me. The stink of my
sores was unbearable, even to me. You came every
day. You washed my wounds. You bandaged them.
You gave much time and patience to me. Only with
those who are well and who don't want to work
do you grumble loudly. One day you said to me,
"Now, Ephé, I will give you a new American medi-
cation against leprosy. The pus will stop running.
Your sores will close. Your poor body will heal
again. You will be able to walk again. You will be
able to preach again your catechism in the villages."

That was how you spoke and how it happened.
First I was able to sleep again because the suffering
was less. The pain was not so terrible any more.
Then the pus stopped running. After three months, I
was healed. And now today I can march from one
village to another. I always come back to you to

show myself, as you told me to. But on your birthday I come not because I want to show myself at the hospital. I come because I want to see you. I want you to know that I pray to the Lord that he keeps you here because we not only need you. We love you.

When the man finished, he looked at the doctor with beaming eyes. Schweitzer embraced him. "I thank you for coming on my birthday," he said. "Yes, you and I, we grew old together. We belong together."

Who of us, even those of us who have studied Schweitzer's life, knew about the great mercy the doctor had shown this one forsaken man for so many years? When I think of him visiting that leper in his misery, cleaning his wounds, changing his bandages, giving him a reason to live, I see Jesus. I picture this man whose body once oozed with sores, and it reminds me of Lazarus, the diseased beggar whose open sores were so disgusting that only the dogs came near him.

It reminds me, too, of the man with leprosy who approached Jesus in Matthew 8:2 and fell down before him, pleading. "Lord, if you want to, you can make me well again." And when I picture Schweitzer saying, "Ephé, my friend, here I am to help you again," I see Jesus touching the leper and saying, "I want to. Be healed!"

As a boy, I loved copies of the Bible that had pictures in them because they brought the stories to life. I think that is what happened that evening at the library. When I saw Schweitzer's face, sweating under a pith helmet, giving his life to so many, the stories about Jesus were brought to life. And when I read the accounts of Schweitzer's compassion for the hurting, I sensed it was Jesus' compassion living in him and working through him. This is what it looks like, the pictures seem to be saying, to live in the world as one who comes not to be served but to serve. These are the steps of the Savior's dance. And to some degree or another, they are the steps of his dance with us.

Other steps in this dance were ones I observed as they swirled around me. They involve two of my daughters and one of my friends.

159

One of my daughters has loved giraffes since she was a child, collecting photographs and replicas over the years, and buying greeting cards with giraffes on the front. A couple of years ago she told us of her desire to go to Africa. She isn't sure whether it will be for weeks or for months or for years. All she is sure of is that someday she will go there. Who knows what Jesus is wanting to do through her there, or what he is wanting to do *for* her?

Another one of my daughters for much of her life has felt deeply about the plight of the African people, especially the children. Last year she married a young man, the son of parents who were medical missionaries in . . . no, not Africa . . . Argentina. At the wedding, though, her in-laws told us they had accepted a call to . . . you guessed it . . . Africa. All their belongings, in fact, had already been sent there.

One evening during the week before my daughter's

wedding, our family was eating a late dinner around the table. We talked together, laughed together, toasted together, and it was one of those emotionally rich, Norman Rockwell moments that will forever hang in my memory. Toward the end of the evening, my daughter talked about her future plans, about her financé's parents going to Africa and the possibility of one day joining them there. She spoke with such hopeful tones, but the more she talked, the more silent I became.

Seeing something of the sadness in my face, she asked, "What's wrong, Dad?"

I couldn't speak; I only shook my head that nothing was wrong.

"You can tell me," she said.

I shook my head no.

"Will you tell me later?"

"Maybe," I said. And it took all my strength to say that one word.

Later that night I went to her room, gave her a hug, and tried to explain the weight of the thoughts I'd had at dinner. The thought of not seeing her for maybe years at a time. The thought of her getting sick over there or needing something and my not being able to help her. The thought of her kids growing up and my not being there to see them.

"Those thoughts were too much to bear," I told her, "and that's why I couldn't talk earlier." We held each other as we cried.

"We're not going right away," she said, trying to console me.

"I know."

"Don't worry, Dad, God will take care of us."

"I know he will. It's still hard."

"It's hard for me, too."

At the wedding reception, she had picked out a song for the band to play and invited me to dance. It was, by God's mercy, a slow dance. When the music stopped, she took her husband's hand to dance with him. It was a different dance, a little faster, a little more contemporary. They were beautiful together. And so was their dance. It was not a dance I could have done, but it perfectly suited them, and they moved through the steps with such grace.

161

Later that year an old friend came into town and invited me to lunch. He had become a Christian at a Young Life camp the year that I was co-leading the club at his high school. He had been an Episcopal priest for a number of years in inner-city Houston, but he told me that recently he had taken a position working with Houston churches in an interdenominational effort to help . . . Africa.

At lunch he showed me a video on his laptop computer of a multiracial rally in a soccer stadium where Christians of all denominations came together in humility, repenting of the sins of the past and renewing their commitment to the future, to love as Christ had loved and to serve as he had served. The two of us watched the video through a mist of tears. My friend's voice cracked as he spoke of what God was doing there. Around his wrist was a red elastic band with the words, "Pray for Africa." I told him I would, that I would pray both for Africa and for him, in whatever role God had for him there.

When I look back on the dance that Jesus has been leading me in, and on the dance he has been leading several of those around me in, the steps seem to be leading in some way to Africa. Is Africa a place that Jesus is leading me? I'm not sure, but this is what I think. I think he has been leading me to a place, not where I would go, necessarily, but where I could *let go*. A place where I could let go of my children . . . and let go of my fears for them.

The Lord led Albert Schweitzer to Africa. That was his dance. Surely his parents had fears about him going there. Somehow, though, in spite of his parents not being there, he managed to sidestep the quicksand and survive the jungle. He escaped being devoured by lions or thrashed by alligators or squeezed to death by boa constrictors. He lived, in fact, to the ripe old age of ninety.

The Lord is still leading people to Africa . . . because it is a place where he still wants to dance. As far as my children are concerned, I believe the Lord will take their hand, draw them close, and reveal where he is leading them. It will be a different dance than he has led me in, a little faster, perhaps, a little more contemporary.

But they will be beautiful together.

So will their dance.

And so will yours. When Jesus draws you into the divine embrace, it is because there is a special and unique dance he wants to do with you. There was a dance he did with Peter, leading him in a ministry with the Jews. There was one he did with Paul, leading him in a ministry with the Gentiles. There was one he did with Schweitzer in Africa. And there is one he is longing to do with you.

Together you will be beautiful.

And oh, the places you will go!

THE CRITICS

OF THE DANCE

A musician was playing on a very beautiful instrument, and the music so enraptured the people that they were driven to dance ecstatically. Then a deaf man who knew nothing of music passed by, and seeing the enthusiastic dancing of the people he decided they must be insane.

THE BAAL SHEM, QUOTED BY ABRAHAM HESCHEL,

GOD IN SEARCH OF MAN: A PHILOSOPHY OF JUDAISM

When the waltz gained popularity in Europe, religious leaders particularly opposed it. They railed against the rapid, turning movements and the close contact of the partners. "A wicked dance," they called it. "Shockingly intimate."

When the waltz was introduced at a ball in London by the Prince Regent in July of 1816, it provoked this scathing editorial in *The Times*: "We remarked with pain that the indecent foreign dance called the Waltz was introduced (we believe for the first time) at the English court on Friday last . . . it is quite sufficient to cast one's eyes on the voluptuous intertwining of the limbs and close compressure on the bodies in their dance, to see that it is indeed far removed from the modest reserve which has hitherto been considered distinctive to English females. So long as this obscene display was confined to prostitutes and adulteresses, we did not think it deserving of notice; but now that it is attempted to be forced on the respectable classes of society by the evil examples of their superiors, we feel it a duty to warn every parent against exposing his daughter to so fatal a contagion."

The reaction to the waltz in the United States was less caustic but still cautious, as can be seen in the advice given in *The Gentleman and Lady's Book of Politeness,* printed in Massachusetts in 1833: "The waltz is a dance of quite too loose a character, and unmarried ladies should refrain from it altogether."

Religious leaders and guardians of good manners were not the only ones critical of the waltz. Dance instructors also opposed it. But their reasons didn't involve manners or morals, they involved money. The more stately court dances, such as the minuet, required long hours of instruction, but the waltz, because of its simple steps, could be learned without professional help, posing a threat to their livelihood. Seeing their students swept away by the popularity of this new dance, they banded together to suppress the movement.

The scribes and Pharisees responded the same way to Jesus' popularity. The dance they taught was equivalent to the minuet, requiring long hours of instruction and tedious routines of practice. Jesus' dance was more like the waltz. "Learn from me," he urged them, in essence, saying, "I am a gentle leader and my steps are easy" (Matthew 11:29-30). So many of them did, that the religious leaders sought to suppress the movement.

They monitored Jesus (see Luke 6:7), confronted him (see Mark 11:28), tried to entrap him (see Luke 20:20-26), plotted to capture him (see Matthew 26:3-5), and then to kill him (see Matthew 27:1). When they

succeeded, they breathed a sigh of relief, thinking the
movement had died with him. But suddenly, unexpectedly, the movement returned to life. The early chapters
of Acts record its resurgence and the attempts of the
religious leaders to stop it.

When the Holy Spirit came, exhilarating things
happened, which critics dismissed as drunkenness,
explaining the phenomena in purely natural terms
(see Acts 2:1-13). Countering the critics, Peter preached
on the divine interpretation of those events, including
the Cross (see verses 14-36). And three thousand people
were drawn into the dance (see verses 41-47).

169

The next two chapters record the first festive steps of
the early church. At every turn there were awesome signs,
miraculous healings, and wonderful conversions. Then,
with Ananias and Sapphira, came a strain of suddenly
somber music, stopping everyone in their tracks (see Acts
5:1-11). Soon, however, the joyful rhythms returned—
crowds of people were coming to faith, throngs of sick
were being healed, scores of the afflicted were being set
free from demonic forces (see verses 12-16).

This time, though, the dance the disciples were
doing prompted more than criticism. It prompted
censorship. Upset by what they were hearing and seeing,
the high priest and his associates silenced the disciples
by throwing them in prison (see verses 17-18). Later
that night, though, an angel came, releasing them. "Go
your way, stand and speak to the people in the temple
the whole message of this Life" (see verses 19-20). Keep
dancing, he seemed to be saying.

When the religious authorities heard the apostles

were footloose in the temple, they brought them back and stood them before the Sanhedrin (see verses 21-27). You are not dancing to the tune we ordered you to dance to, the high priest said, in essence (see verse 28). And in essence, Peter and the other apostles told him, We dance to a different tune, to a higher and greater tune, and that is why we're not dancing to yours (see verses 29-32).

In *Walden,* Thoreau says, "If a man does not keep pace with his companions, perhaps it is because he hears a different drummer. Let him step to the music which he hears, however measured or far away." When Jesus walked the earth, his spiritual ear seemed tuned to the divine orchestrations that were going on around him. In order to hear that music more clearly, he often slipped away to a quiet place by himself. He spent an entire night in prayer, for instance, before he chose his disciples. Later, when the clamor of the crowds became deafening, he withdrew to a lonely place to pray. And the night of his betrayal, when he trembled at the steps that lay before him, he went to a secluded garden to quiet the voice of his fears so he could hear the distant rhythms of his Father's heart. There he prayed for the strength to step to that music, however his Father had measured it, however hard it was to understand it.

170

Jesus lived his life like that, stepping to the music he heard, which often put him out of step with those around him. For three-and-a-half years the disciples had observed how Jesus lived, noting how intently he listened to God and how simply and humbly and obediently he followed the steps that had been ordained for him. When Jesus left the disciples, he gave them the Holy Spirit as a tuning device, so to speak, to help them home in on the divine orchestration of events so they could become partners in the dance that was going on within them and around them.

Because the apostles were in step with this music, at every turn they were stepping on the toes of the religious establishment, who were deaf to it. When three thousand others were drawn into the dance, they were not only stepping on toes, they were taking center stage. Which infuriated the religious leaders. And they tried to put a stop to it. Why? Because of moral concerns? No. Because of theological differences? No. Because of procedural questions? No.

171

Their motivation was jealousy. The text says they were "filled" with it (Acts 5:17). By nature we are territorial creatures, whether that territory is a dating relationship or a donor base. When our territory is threatened, a self-protective instinct rushes to suppress the threat. In the natural world, our competitive nature has helped us to survive. In the spiritual world, though, mere survival—whether it is the survival of a relationship or a business or a ministry or even of our physical existence—isn't the highest of heavenly concerns. When Jesus was baptizing in Judea and John was baptizing in Aenon, so many people flocked to where Jesus was that John's disciples came to him, voicing concern over their dwindling numbers (see John 3:22-26). John, however, wasn't the least concerned, because he knew he had been called to a dance, not to a dance competition. "He must increase," John said, speaking of

Jesus, "but I must decrease" (verse 30). John was so in tune with the divine orchestrations of events that he knew his place on the dance floor as well as the steps to the dance that God had ordained for him. And not one of those steps was a competitive one or even a self-protective one.

———————————

Those enraptured by the music are driven to dance.

Those deaf to the music are driven to critique the dance of others.

The voice of the critic, especially within our peer group, exerts a powerful force not only on the way we think but also on the way we act. Peer pressure is essentially the fear of the critic, whether that critic is one intimidating person or the collective intimidation of the entire group.

The most compelling study I have read on the power of peer pressure is the book *Ordinary Men,* by Christopher R. Browning. The book analyzes the behavior of the men of Reserve Police Battalion 101 in Germany during the Second World War. Too old or too weak to fight in the war, the men had been conscripted for special service behind the lines. They were not Nazis. They were not worshipers of Hitler. They were not racial fanatics. They were ordinary men—middle-age, working-class men: a forty-year-old barber, for example, a thirty-seven-year-old tailor, a thirty-five-year-old metalworker. They were family men, too, with wives and children. By all appearances, decent, upstanding citizens.

The five hundred men in the battalion were sent to Poland, where for three weeks they stayed in a school building in a small town, awaiting their first assignment. On the morning of July 13, 1942, the assignment came. In the predawn darkness, they boarded a convoy of trucks loaded with ammunition. They were not told where they were going or what would be required of them once they arrived. Jostled over rough terrain for more than an hour and a half, they came to the outskirts of the village of Józefów, where the convoy stopped. The first colors of dawn revealed modest, peasant homes with thatched roofs, a typical Polish village. And typical of such villages, the population was mixed, including eighteen hundred Jews.

173

As the village slept, the men of Reserve Police Battalion 101 quietly got out of their trucks and gathered around their commander, awaiting orders. With his voice cracking and tears filling his eyes, the commander told them they were orders he didn't like, orders he regretted having to carry out, but they had come from his superiors and must be obeyed.

The male Jews, he told them, were to be separated from the rest and sent to a work camp. The remaining Jews were to be shot. Women, children, the elderly, they were all to be shot. His face was pale as he spoke. Visibly shaken, he told the older men they could opt out of the mission if they didn't feel up to it. One man stepped forward. Then another. Out of five hundred men, though, only twelve opted out.

By nightfall, these ordinary men with ordinary jobs and ordinary families had completed their mission.

They had rounded up all the Jews in the village and separated them, sending three hundred to a work camp and shooting the other fifteen hundred.

In the sixteen months following that massacre, the men of Reserve Police Battalion 101 sent forty-five thousand Jews to the gas chambers of Treblinka and shot at least thirty-eight thousand others, for a total of eighty-three thousand deaths.

Why did they do it? Why did such ordinary men commit such atrocities?

Some stated they were merely following orders. Others said they felt they were releasing their victims from their misery, especially the children. But these were not the main reasons. In studying the post-war interrogations of 210 of these mass murderers, the author learned that the main reasons were peer pressure and careerism. The men feared what the others would think if they didn't participate, feared being looked at as weak or cowardly. They also feared the repercussions to their careers if they didn't participate, thinking that after the war they might be passed over for promotion or their businesses boycotted.

The author concludes his book with these haunting words: "Within virtually every social collective, the peer group exerts tremendous pressures on behavior and sets moral norms. If the men of Reserve Police Battalion 101 could become killers under such circumstances, what group of men cannot?"

The research is not only compelling but is corroborated by numerous examples in the Scriptures. Look at the pressure the different peer groups exerted at Christ's trial and crucifixion. Look at the high priest and his associates, for example, who ruthlessly interrogated Jesus. Or the cohort of Roman soldiers, who savagely beat him. Or Pilate, who caved in to the pressure of the crowd that was chanting for Jesus to be crucified. Or the throng of people around the cross, who relentlessly mocked him.

Individually, they were, for the most part, ordinary men. Yet collectively, they were responsible for extraordinary injustices and cruelties. In his sermon "The Inner Ring," C. S. Lewis talks about the desire we all have to be a part of a group, some inner ring of membership. "Of all passions," he writes, "the passion for the Inner Ring is most skillful in making a man who is not yet very bad do very bad things."

175

Someone once said that the only thing necessary for evil to triumph is for good men to do nothing. Peer pressure is the reason why good men did nothing that dark night in Jerusalem when evil triumphed. Joseph of Arimathea, a good man and a member of the Sanhedrin, did nothing. He had become a follower of Jesus, but a secret one, we are told, for fear of the Jews. Even as good a man and as openly committed a follower as Peter crumbled under the peer pressure of those around the campfire the night of Christ's arrest.

Peer pressure is something we commonly associate with the tyranny of our teenage years, indigenous to middle schools and high schools. But it isn't confined there. Its presence is pervasive. In seminaries as well as state colleges. In ministries as well as fraternities. In elder boards as well as corporate boards.

How do we escape the power of peer pressure, the power of the critic that inhibits us from the divine embrace?

The answer to that question can be found in the Roman Colosseum.

The Colosseum stands as a monument to our baser nature. During the time of the Roman Empire, crowds gathered early to get the best seats, where they watched and cheered as wild animals tore prisoners of the empire to shreds, where combatants fought to the death, and where great battles were staged to replicate victories on the frontier. Vanquished gladiators, slaves, prisoners, and Christians were among the victims.

Ignatius, a disciple of John and later bishop of Antioch, was one of the many Christians who was taken prisoner. He was sent to Rome in A.D. 107 and condemned to death for promoting Christianity. After his sentencing, one of the emperor's representatives offered him freedom if he would recant and make sacrifices to the Roman gods. Ignatius replied, "By your bland words you wish to deceive and destroy me. Know that this mortal life has no attraction for me; I wish to go to Jesus, who is the bread of immortality and the drink of eternal life. I live entirely for Him, and my soul yearns for Him. I despise all your torments, and I cast at your feet your proffered liberty."

Enraged, the official pronounced his verdict: "Let him be bound, and let loose two lions to devour him."

How did Ignatius overcome the intimidation of the Roman government and the fear of a horrible death before an arena full of bloodthirsty onlookers? He had experienced something that they never had. The love of Jesus. And he had experienced it so deeply that it created in him such a yearning that nothing on earth attracted him.

Not the enticements of a career.

Not the acceptance of a crowd.

And not the approval of a critic.

If Ignatius teaches us anything, it is this: The fear of criticism is silenced by falling in love. If we fall in love with Jesus, not only will nothing on this earth attract us, nothing on this earth will intimidate us.

177

THE INFORMALITY
OF THE DANCE

I think perfectionism is based on the obsessive belief that if you run carefully enough, hitting each stepping-stone just right, you won't have to die. The truth is that you will die anyway and that a lot of people who aren't even looking at their feet are going to do a whole lot better than you, and have a lot more fun while they're doing it.

ANNE LAMOTT, *BIRD BY BIRD:*

SOME INSTRUCTIONS ON WRITING AND LIFE

B rowsing the shelves for audio books to keep me company on a long trip, I came across the title *Word by Word.* Thinking they were tapes for building a better vocabulary, I pinched the spine of the vinyl album and pulled it from the shelf. The summary on the case revealed the tapes were not about words but about writing.

"By Anne Lamott."

Never heard of her, was my first thought, but the title intrigued me, so I added her to my stack of traveling companions.

Of all the tapes I brought with me, she proved to be the best company. Alternating between Woody Allen moments of self-deprecation and drive-by criticisms of politicians, Lamott's style was as delightful as it was disarming. The tape was a jeans-and-T-shirt version of her book *Bird by Bird.* It was not a stiffly read text like so many nonfiction tapes, but was more casual. The tape led me to the book, which is subtitled, appropriately, "Some Instructions on Writing and Life."

"Good writing is about telling the truth," Lamott writes. She is a good writer, and she tells the truth of her story with unflinching candor. I fell in love not only with her truthfulness but also with her playfulness. Because of that, I went looking for other books she had written.

In *Traveling Mercies,* she invites the reader along for the wild ride that is her spiritual journey, taking us down the detours, the dead ends, and the U-turns. At first we're not sure where she's taking us, but with the wind in our faces and the open road ahead, we're enjoying the ride so much we don't really care.

At times, her thoughts are irreverent, and we find ourselves laughing at them the way we might laugh at a joke that is in such poor taste but at the same time so side-splittingly funny we can't help it. At other times, her thoughts are so reverent that the air stills in their presence.

I am thinking of the time her pastor, the Reverend Ms. Veronica Goines, told a story to the congregation one Sunday at the predominantly black Presbyterian church Lamott attends in Marin County, California. The church has been for her a sanctuary in the deepest sense of the word. It has been a place of refuge, a place of rest, and a place where she and her son have returned, week after week, missing only about ten Sundays in the twelve years they have attended. The story the pastor told the congregation happened when she was about seven years old, when her best friend wandered away from the neighborhood and got lost:

The little girl ran up and down the streets of the big town where they lived, but she couldn't find a single landmark. She was very frightened. Finally a policeman stopped to help her. He put her in the passenger seat of his car, and they drove around until she finally saw her church. She pointed it out to the policeman, and then she told him firmly, "You could let me out now. This is my church, and I can always find my way home from here."

"And that is why I have stayed so close to mine," Lamott comments, "because no matter how bad I am feeling, how lost or lonely or frightened, when I see the faces of the people at my church, and hear their tawny voices, I can always find my way home."

183

Much of Lamott's life was spent trying to find her way home. She slept around, drank heavily, and, in her own words, snorted cocaine "like an anteater." In the spring of 1984, she found herself pregnant from a relationship with a married man. She did not love him, nor did she want to have a child, let alone *his* child. A friend of hers took her to get an abortion. She came home from the clinic feeling such enormous sadness that its presence was almost palpable. She tried to push away the sadness with pain pills the doctor had given her, washing them down with alcohol, drinking through the night, through the darkness and the loneliness and the pain. Night after night, she continued this ritual of remorse. By the seventh night, she noticed she was bleeding. For a time it was profuse. Hours later, the bleeding stopped. Exhausted, she crawled back in bed, waiting for the dawn, frightened and alone and disgusted with herself. Trembling, she turned off the light. As she lay there, a strange sense of someone else's presence came over her. She turned on the light by her bed. Nothing. Her suddenly sober eyes searched every shadowy recess of the room. Still nothing. Finally, she turned off the light. After a while, the presence returned. This time she knew who it was. It was Jesus. She felt him sitting in her bedroom loft, hunched in the corner.

Her response to such a sacred moment?

"I was appalled," she wrote. "I thought about my life and my brilliant hilarious progressive friends, I thought about what everyone would think of me if I became a Christian, and it seemed an utterly impossible thing that simply could not be allowed to happen. I turned to the wall and said out loud, 'I would rather die.'"

Jesus said nothing in reply. He just sat there in the corner, she said, "watching me with patience and love."

The experience haunted her throughout the next morning. She tried to dismiss it. After all, she hadn't actually *seen* anything. Or *heard* anything. It was just a sensation. Who knows, maybe it was guilt-induced. Or alcohol-induced. Or maybe the loss of blood contributed to it. "But then," she wrote, "everywhere I went, I had the feeling that a little cat was following me, wanting me to reach down and pick it up, wanting me to open the door and let it in. But I knew what would happen: you let a cat in one time, give it a little milk, and then it stays forever. So I tried to keep one step ahead of it, slamming my houseboat door when I entered or left."

The next Sunday, she went back to the church she had been visiting. The other times she had stayed only for the music. This time, though, she was too hungover to even stand during the singing. She ended up sitting there when it was over and staying for the sermon. The preacher's words seemed ridiculous to her. But the song that closed the service was, in her words, "so deep and pure and raw that I could not escape. . . . I felt like their voices or *something* was rocking me in its bosom, holding me like a scared kid, and I opened up to that feeling—and it washed over me."

She slipped out before the service ended, weeping as she ran. All the while she felt the presence of that little cat, running after her. Eventually she tired, and her pace slowed. By the time she came to her houseboat, she stopped at the door, stood there a minute, then hung her head, blurted out an expletive, then sighed: "I quit." She took a deep breath and said: "All right. You can come in."

185

And that, as she put it, "was my beautiful moment of conversion."

That is her story, and she tells it bravely. If it were my story, or your story, though, I wonder if you or I would have the courage to stand up in church and tell it? Or if we did, I wonder if the church would have the courage to hear it?

There is no room in the inn of many churches where we can share such stories. If there is, it is likely a small room, one that is meticulously kept and carefully watched. Consequently, we find ourselves with stories we can't truly tell at church, secrets we can't really share, burdens we can't fully lay down. Frederick Buechner, in his book *Whistling in the Dark,* explains why:

> Alcoholics Anonymous or A.A. is the name of a group of men and women who acknowledge that addiction to alcohol is ruining their lives. Their purpose in coming together is to give it up and help others do the same. They realize they can't pull this off by themselves. They believe they need each other, and they believe they need God. The ones who aren't so sure about God speak instead of their Higher Power. . . .
>
> Nobody lectures them, and they do not lecture each other. They simply tell their own stories with the candor that anonymity makes possible. They tell where they went wrong and how day by day they are trying to go right. They tell where they find the strength and understanding and hope to keep trying. Sometimes one of them will take special responsibility for another—to be available at any hour of day or night if the need arises. There's not much more to it than that, and it seems to be enough. Healing happens. Miracles are made.
>
> You can't help thinking that something like this is what the Church is meant to be and maybe once was before it got to be Big Business. Sinners Anonymous. "I can will what is right but I cannot do it," is the way Saint Paul put it, speaking for all of us. "For I do not do the good I want, but the evil I do not want is what I do" (Romans 7:18-19, RSV). . . .

No matter what far place alcoholics end up in, either in this country or virtually anywhere else, they know that there will be an A.A. meeting nearby to go to and that at that meeting they will find strangers who are not strangers to help and to heal, to listen to the truth and to tell it. That is what the Body of Christ is all about.

Would it ever occur to Christians in a far place to turn to a Church nearby in hope of finding the same? Would they find it? If not, you wonder what is so Big about the Church's Business.

187

I wonder myself sometimes. And I wonder if Jesus were to come back, would he be as impressed with all that goes on at church as we sometimes are? The New Testament uses different metaphors to describe the church and how it was meant to operate. A family is one of them. And a body, another. But a business? Never. Yet the way the church has evolved, it seems closer to the image of a business than to a body or a family.

The church of my youth was not big business. It was, however, very formal business. Part of that was due to the times I grew up in. Part of it was the place.

I grew up in Texas during the 1950s. On Sundays, virtually every store closed except the grocery store. Groceries were a necessity—or so the Blue Laws declared—and therefore could be sold on the Sabbath. Other things, like laundry detergent or light bulbs, could not. I still remember going into the grocery store on Sundays and seeing entire aisles covered with tarps to mark them off-limits. Or being told at the checkout counter, "I'm sorry, but you can't buy that on Sunday," and then the cashier putting it aside. You couldn't buy toys on Sunday. Or comic books. And, for a while, anyway, you couldn't buy soft drinks or candy.

Not exactly the type of legislation that endears a kid to religion.

Kids couldn't go outside and play on Sundays, at least not in our neighborhood. I never understood why. One of our neighbors was a Presbyterian minister, and maybe that was a part of it. His oldest son was my best friend, and he never played outside on Sunday. If we were allowed to play, it had to be either inside or in the back-yard, where we were always hushed if we got too loud.

We couldn't do a lot of things on Sunday, but of course we could go to church.

Getting ready for church seemed an instructional page torn from a book on medieval torture. We were fussed over on Sunday mornings, with Mom trimming our nails to the quick, leaving the tips of our fingers tender and throbbing.

"Ow, ow, ow!"

She scoured our faces with a washcloth, then used it like a grub hoe to dig in our ears. "You've got potatoes growing in there," she would explain.

"Ouch!" we would say, flinching and squirming.

Next came the hair oil.

Then . . . the brush.

The brush had long, stiff bristles that furrowed the scalp.

"That hurts, that hurts! Ouch!"

Then came the clothes.

"Sunday clothes," as they were called. Women wore dresses with matching handbags, white gloves, and often hats with veils. Men wore suits with white shirts and ties. And no one cut a break for a kid. We had to wear slacks and pressed white shirts with the top button choking our necks and freshly shined shoes that cramped our toes. The only break we ever got was the invention of the clip-on tie.

Then there was the drive.

We attended a Lutheran church on the other side of town, and the drive was long and hot and sweaty. By the time we got there, we were wilted. In the sanctuary, I sat next to my parents in hard wooden pews, where I drew on the bulletin with one of the pencils provided in the back of the pew. The hymns were all ancient and mostly unfamiliar, with the exceptions of "A Mighty Fortress Is Our God" and "Beautiful Savior." We usually sang every stanza, even of the songs that nobody knew, some of which not even the organist knew.

189

We stood up a lot as we sang those hymns. Other times we were motioned to be seated, which was always a relief. We stood up and sat down a lot in church. It served to keep the blood flowing, which I guess was good because it kept everyone awake longer. We stood for whatever creed was being recited that day, and for the Lord's Prayer, and for any one of the numerous other lesser liturgies.

Once the sermon started, I got comfortable on the pew, leaning my head against Dad's shoulder or resting it on Mom's lap, where I often fell asleep.

The Lutheran service was appropriately reverent, which my mother insisted wasn't true of the Baptists. Baptists spoke in their sanctuary, even laughed and carried on with each other before and after the service. We didn't do that in our church. Everything was hushed and restrained. People were polite but not chummy.

I do not have horror stories about my church experience, as some people do. Nobody ever yelled at me. Nobody ever slapped my hands with a ruler. Nobody ever made me grovel for penance. All the while, though, a subliminal message was being communicated that I don't think was healthy: *Come to church, but come cleaned-up, with your best clothes, your best posture, your best face, and keep your secrets and your sadness at home, where they belong.*

I don't think the early church was like that. I think it was a place where people came as they were, slaves and freemen, sitting side by side, laying down their burdens; Greek and Jew, elbow to elbow, sharing their heartaches; male and female, revealing not only the dark secrets of how they went astray, but also the luminous secrets of how Jesus pursued them, found them, and carried them home.

190

The people of the early church were desperate people, for the most part, living in desperate times. They were less likely to be pillars of the community and more likely to be prostitutes; less likely to be aristocrats and more likely to be adulterers; less likely to come from the city's social register and more likely to come from the ranks of the diseased, the demon-possessed, and the down-and-out. Imagine the stories they had to tell. And imagine how the freedom to tell their stories brought freedom to so many who heard them.

Room was made in the service of the early church both for the Holy Spirit and for the holiness of their own stories. And in the dim light and dirty mess of such a stable, divine things were given birth.

What about the church of today? Is something miraculous being birthed there, or simply mass-produced? How did the business of the church get to be so big and so formal?

191

The evolution of the church is mirrored in the evolution of the waltz, and that image, I believe, reflects not only who we are but how we got that way.

The word *waltz* comes from the German word *walzen,* which means "to roll, turn, or glide." It was a whirling, gliding, turning folk dance where enraptured couples entwined themselves with each other, clapping to the music and kicking up their heels. More than any other dance, the waltz embodied the joyous spontaneity of romantic abandon. If the waltz was anything, it was passionate. Filled with longing. Overflowing with joy. And renewing the spirit. As one dance manual put it: "Never before had the man clasped the lady to him in a facing position with his arm around her waist and rotated round the ballroom in what was almost an embrace; and rarely, if ever, had the dancers appeared to be dancing for their own pleasure as opposed to providing entertainment for admiring onlookers."

These early folk dances were the communal participations of the peasantry. Many of the familiar waltz tunes can be traced back to simple peasant yodeling melodies. Descending the alpine regions of Austria and Bavaria, this music filled the beer gardens of Vienna in the 1700s, spilling onto the banks of the Danube in rural inns and taverns, where bands of roving musicians boarded riverboats and spread the revelry of the waltz wherever they went.

The waltz later made its way into the ballrooms of society, and in 1787, it was brought to the operatic stage in Vienna, becoming not only a respectable business but also big business. Professional dance troupes replaced the peasants. Simple rural clothes gave way to long flowing gowns and impeccably tailored suits. Beer and bratwurst gave way to champagne and caviar. Fiddlers gave way to full orchestras. And open grassy meadows gave way to polished ballroom floors.

In a similar way, the church evolved from a simple folk dance into a staged performance. In many places where professionals took the stage, formality replaced spontaneity, precision replaced passion, restraint replaced revelry. Relegated to the audience, the peasants sat and watched. And the more they watched, the more they expected the professionals to entertain them. To please the increasingly critical audience, the performance became driven by perfectionism.

Which is what drives a lot of churches today.

A church driven by perfectionism is a church driven to distraction. It's Martha in the kitchen, not Mary seated at the Savior's feet.

"Perfectionism," writes Anne Lamott, "is the voice of the oppressor, the enemy of the people. It will keep you cramped and insane your whole life." The perfectionism that is driving the church and other Christian organizations is oppressive. For the people who put on the performance, it is keeping them cramped and insane. And for the people who sit in the audience, it's making them critical.

I got a chance to see the price that perfectionism exacts from a church, both from its staff and from its members, one weekend when I was speaking at a retreat. After my last message, a man asked if he could talk about something that had happened in a church he had recently left. I could tell by the look on his face that he was distraught. He related to me how he had been on the staff of a large, progressive church, where he ministered to a group of people with cerebral palsy, some severely disabled and all wheelchair bound. He had been asked to give a presentation for one of the Sunday services, describing the group and his ministry with them. He told his class, and they were excited about getting on stage to share something of their story and something of the secret of who they were. When the man shared his idea for the presentation with the staff, they flinched at the thought of having people with such severe disabilities on public display. They felt it would make the audience feel uncomfortable. As a compromise, they asked the man to videotape the class instead. He was instructed to be careful not to show the people rocking back and forth in their wheelchairs, which might be off-putting to see, but rather to focus more on their faces.

He went back to the class and explained to them, as delicately as he could, the change of plans. Although disappointed, they agreed. When the man submitted the video, he was told by the person in charge of quality control for the service that it didn't meet the church's production values, and because of that, couldn't be shown. The man was devastated. He pleaded with the person, told him how important it was for the church body to honor the weaker members among them, and how it would crush the people in his class who had put so much work into the project. The person in charge wouldn't budge. The man then appealed to the staff, but the staff stood up for high standards and against anything that didn't measure up to them.

Many of those in the class were so hurt they left the church. When they did, the minister turned in his resignation. He came to me, his voice at times trembling, wondering if he had done the right thing.

I could hardly believe the story, hardly believe the insensitivity of that church staff, let alone the cruelty. Do they see who they have become? Do they know how far out of step they are with the Lord Jesus, whose life was lived among the lame and the leper and the epileptic?

The church service went on as usual, without the jarring images of bodies contorting in wheelchairs or the distracting sounds of slurred speech. I'm sure everything that Sunday went perfectly. But at what cost?

According to an ancient Chinese proverb, "One may judge of a king by the state of dancing during his reign." A provocative thought, which raises a lot of "what ifs." What if the pastor of a church or the president of a

194

parachurch organization wasn't judged by his performance, at least not in the way we most often judge performance? What if he wasn't judged by how perfect Sunday mornings were? What if he wasn't judged by the number of dollars raised during his term? or by the numbers of people in attendance? What if he wasn't judged by the state of the budget? or the state of the building program? or the state of the membership drive?

What if he were judged solely by "the state of dancing during his reign." By how dearly the people in his care love Jesus. By how longingly they listen for the rhythms of Christ's heart. And by how willingly they follow the steps he is leading them in.

What if his main role was to help the people entrusted to his care to cultivate a more intimate relationship with Christ? To incorporate into the job description of every staff member regularly scheduled times of retreat—daily, weekly, monthly, yearly times to get alone with the Lord Jesus, sitting at his feet, beholding the beauty of his face and listening to the gentleness of his voice. Imagine individuals doing this, couples, entire families, cultivating the still point of the dance. Imagine the times when they would get together to share what they'd seen, what they'd heard. Imagine an entire community of people living like that. Adoring Jesus. Longing for him. Listening to him. And moving in step not only with him but with each other.

Imagine it.

The state of dancing.

What a state that would be . . . and how wonderful to be a part of it!

THE END
OF THE DANCE

And now I'm glad I didn't know
The way it all would end
The way it all would go
Our lives are better left to chance
I could have missed the pain,
But I'd of had to miss the dance.

GARTH BROOKS, "THE DANCE"

S ometimes the uncertainty of life is scary; we don't
know exactly where we're going or how our life is
going to end up. It would help to have the sheet music.
It would take a lot of the stress out of life. The sheet
music is what the disciples wanted when they asked,
"Who of us will be the greatest in the kingdom of
heaven?" Or when they said, "We have left everything
to follow you! What then will there be for us?"

The bad news is, the Emperor doesn't offer us the
sheet music.

The good news is, he offers us his hand.

He doesn't ask that we memorize the music or
choreograph the dance. He simply asks that we place
our hand in his and trust him for the next step. That
is what he did with the disciples just before his ascen-
sion. Before Jesus left to be with his Father, he revealed
the next step in the dance. He told the disciples not to
leave Jerusalem but to wait there for the Holy Spirit
(see Acts 1:1-5).

Curious where all this was leading, they asked him,

"Lord, is it at this time You are restoring the kingdom to Israel?"

"It is not for you to know times or epochs which the Father has fixed by His own authority," Jesus answered. It's not important for you to know that far into the future, he seemed to be saying, but I will tell you what to expect in the next step and where that step will take you. "You shall receive power when the Holy Spirit has come upon you; and you shall be My witnesses both in Jerusalem, and in all Judea and Samaria, and even to the remotest part of the earth" (Acts 1: 6-8).

Only rarely does Jesus reveal the end of our individual dance, the way he informed Peter of the pain and suffering that awaited him at the end of his life (see John 21:18-22). He has, however, revealed the end of the dance for all of human history. He entrusted the revelation to John, who wrote what he saw in the best words he had. The book of Revelation reads like a fairy tale, with its punishment of evildoers and reward of the righteous, with its golden streets and jeweled walls, with the banishment of darkness and the glory of the Lord illumining everything. Like a fairy tale, it seems too good to be true. And yet it is true.

The love for fairy tales is universal. In his essay "Sometimes Fairy Stories," C. S. Lewis explains why he particularly liked the genre: "I thought I saw how stories of this kind could steal past a certain inhibition which had paralysed much of my own religion in childhood. Why did one find it so hard to feel as one was told one ought to feel about God or about the sufferings of Christ? I thought the chief reason was that one was told one ought to. An obligation to feel can freeze feelings. And reverence itself did harm. The whole subject was associated with lower voices; almost as if it were something medical. But supposing that by casting all these things into an imaginary world, stripping them of their stained-glass and Sunday school associations, one could make them for the first time appear in their real potency? Could one not thus steal past those watchful dragons? I thought one could."

Lewis succeeded in stealing past those watchful dragons in a series of seven children's books known as The Chronicles of Narnia. The first volume was published in England in October 1950. The U.S. version made its debut a month later, which was two months after I was born. My mother read to me as a child, but when I was old enough to read on my own, what I read mostly were comic books and Hardy Boys mysteries and books with lots of pictures of sharks and dinosaurs and such. I was in college before I ever heard of C. S. Lewis, and then what attracted me were his theological works like *Mere Christianity* and *The Problem of Pain.* I did not read any of his children's books until I had children of my own and began reading to them at night before tucking them into bed.

From time to time I am asked, of all the books I have read over the course of my life, which have meant the most to me. Two stand out. One is Harper Lee's novel, *To Kill a Mockingbird.* The other is C. S. Lewis's Chronicles of Narnia. Forced to choose between the

201

two, I would pick the Chronicles, I think. I would pick them for a number of reasons, but the most important reason is that they aroused in me a yearning for heaven.

Since childhood, I have believed in heaven. I believed it was a real place and hoped that someday I would go there. I heard, however, that you have to die to get there, and not being very much interested in doing that very soon, I was not eager to make the trip.

There were other reasons for my reluctance. It seemed a vague, cloudy place, sedate and serious, from what I could piece together. And ponderously slow. I could never imagine running in heaven, which as a young boy I enjoyed immensely. And if there were no running, it was inconceivable to me that there would be any playing. The two seemed so intertwined that I could not, in my child's mind, separate them. Of course, if you go to church long enough, or to seminary, you get a fuller picture of heaven. Still, it wasn't church that stirred my longing for heaven. And it wasn't seminary. It was a fairy tale.

The first book published in the series was *The Lion, the Witch, and the Wardrobe,* set during World War II at the estate of an old professor who had agreed to house four children from London in his country home until the war was over. Shortly after England declared war on Germany, London evacuated as many of its children as possible to spare them from the terrors and danger of air raids.

Lewis and his housekeeper, Mrs. Moore, lived in Oxford on an eight-acre estate called The Kilns. The beautiful grounds had a pond, a garden, a sprawling meadow with all sorts of adventurous ravines, and was bordered by a thick wall of fir trees. Over the course of the war, a number of children stayed at The Kilns, and each in some way or another had a hand in shaping Lewis's characters. The children in the story are Peter, Susan, Edmund, and Lucy, who stumble upon an enchanted wardrobe in the professor's home that leads to the magical land of Narnia. This land, they discover, is ruled by the White Witch, who has placed a spell on the land so that it is "always winter, but never Christmas." But the true ruler of Narnia, the lion Aslan, has been roused, and everywhere there are traces of a thaw and the coming of spring.

203

When the children finally meet Aslan, Edmund has already been enticed by the witch to join her ranks. With the promise of taking his rightful place to rule at her side, Edmund betrays his brother and sisters. Later in the story, the witch turns on the boy and arranges to have him executed. When Aslan tries to get the witch to release Edmund, she trumps his request by reminding him of the "deep magic" they had agreed upon before the dawn of time. "Every traitor belongs to me as my lawful prey," she sneers. "For every treachery I have a right to a kill."

To free the boy, Aslan offers to be killed in Edmund's place. The witch and all her evil court are elated at the offer. A time and place for Aslan's sacrifice are determined—at night at the Hill of the Stone Table. Here, Aslan is on his way to that fateful hill with Susan and Lucy walking by his side:

"Oh, children, children. Here you must stop. And whatever happens, do not let yourselves be seen. Farewell."

And both the girls cried bitterly (though they hardly knew why) and clung to the Lion and kissed his mane and his nose and his paws and his great, sad eyes. Then he turned from them and walked out onto the top of the hill. And Lucy and Susan, crouching in the bushes, looked after him and this is what they saw.

A great crowd of people were standing all round the Stone Table and though the moon was shining many of them carried torches which burned with evil-looking red flames and black smoke. But such people! Ogres with monstrous teeth, and wolves, and bull-headed men; spirits of evil trees and poisonous plants . . .

A howl and a gibber of dismay went up from the creatures when they first saw the great Lion pacing toward them, and for a moment the Witch herself seemed to be struck with fear. Then she recovered herself and gave a wild, fierce laugh.

"The fool!" she cried. "The fool has come. Bind him fast. . . . "

The hags made a dart at him and shrieked with triumph when they found that he made no resistance at all. Then others—evil dwarfs and apes—rushed in to help them and between them they rolled the huge Lion round on his back and tied all his four paws together, shouting and cheering as if they had done something brave, though, had the

Lion chosen, one of those paws could have been the death of them all. But he made no noise, even when the enemies, straining and tugging, pulled the cords so tight that they cut into his flesh. Then they began to drag him toward the Stone Table.

"Stop!" said the Witch. "Let him first be shaved."

The scene is dark, fiendish, and full of evil. The grotesque gathering, I believe, captures the atmosphere of the torchlit night on which Jesus was betrayed and of the torturous next day when he was crucified. As the moment of Aslan's execution draws near, the forces of evil are emboldened.

Four Hags, holding four torches, stood at the corners of the Table. The Witch bared her arms as she had bared them the previous night when it had been Edmund instead of Aslan. Then she began to whet her knife. It looked to the children, when the gleam of the torchlight fell on it, as if the knife were made of stone not of steel, and it was of a strange and evil shape.

At last she drew near. She stood by Aslan's head. Her face was working and twitching with passion, but his looked up at the sky, still quiet, neither angry nor afraid, but a little sad. Then, just before she gave the blow, she stooped down and said in a quivering voice,

"And now, who has won? Fool, did you think that by all this you would save the human traitor? Now I will kill you instead of him as our pact was, and so the Deep Magic will be appeased. But when you are dead what will prevent me from killing him as well? And who will take him out of my hand *then?* Understand that you have given me Narnia forever, you have lost your own life, and you have not saved his. In that knowledge, despair and die."

The children, we are told, covered their eyes at the unbearable moment of Aslan's death. The scene is so brutal and the presence of evil so tangible, it's hard not to, even as a reader. I have read these passages to small groups before sharing Communion, and it is hard for me to read them without my voice cracking, my hands trembling, and my eyes welling with tears.

The story of Christ's crucifixion is one that many of us have heard in some form or another since childhood. If we have gone to church very much over the years, we've heard it a lot. Even if we have just popped in on Christmas and Easter to pay our respects, we've heard the story. Our familiarity with the story doesn't breed contempt, but it does breed complacency, often inhibiting us from feeling about Christ's crucifixion the way we should feel. Which is why the fairy tale works so well. It steals past our complacency with new images and atmospheres.

Imagine the atmosphere at the Cross. Like the Hill at the Stone Table, Calvary had the full attention of the forces of evil. Satan was there, certainly, along with his grotesque cadre of henchmen. Imagine the brutality of the soldiers, the tauntings of the rabble around the cross, the curses of the criminals on either side. Imagine the humiliation of Christ's nakedness. The degradation. And then the darkness. The three hours of darkness. The aloneness. The abandonment. And the full weight of the world's sin pulling against the nails.

If we had been there, we would have been like the two girls following Aslan, full of fear, finding everything that's happening too horrible to believe, closing our eyes at it. The problem is, we don't go there. And the Good Friday sermons and the Easter pageants often don't take us there to be with those who saw the terrible things they saw, heard the terrible things they heard.

But Lewis takes us there, to see it all, hear it all, feel it all.

Love is what drew Susan and Lucy to the place of Aslan's execution. Love is what drew John and Mary to the place of Christ's crucifixion. And love is what will draw *us* there, time and time again.

The steps of the dance all lead to the Cross.

At the Cross we see how Jesus lost his life and something of how we are to lose ours. It was his responsibility to die. It was the Father's responsibility to resurrect him. To us has been given a similar responsibility. Not to bring life out of death. But to die. Our responsibility is to surrender. The result of our surrender is not our responsibility. Understanding the truth of that has been liberating. It has also been sobering, because dying is the ultimate surrender of control, not only in the physical sense, but also in the daily dying to self that we are all called to do.

What if in our daily lives we started living like Jesus

did? —dying to ourselves, giving of ourselves, surrendering ourselves.

But what happens if we do and God doesn't come through for us? What if he overlooks our surrender? What if he doesn't resurrect those moments of faith when we place the results in his hands, to do with what he pleases, when he pleases? What then?

Then we wait in the tomb another day.

And another, if necessary.

For as many days as God appoints.

Because our days are in *his* hands, not ours. He appoints them all—the day of our birth, the day of our death, and the day of our resurrection. And not only the day of our physical resurrection, but also all the other resurrections of the daily deaths to which we surrender ourselves—those days are in his hands, as well.

Not only are the days of our lives in God's hands, but also the shaping of our lives. All these incremental surrenderings of self are part of the process God uses in shaping us into the image of his son. Jesus was a man of sorrows, we are told. That was part of his beauty. *Our* sorrows acquaint us with *his* sorrows. Apart from suffering, there is a part of Jesus we cannot know. If there is a part of him we cannot know, there is a part of him we cannot love. And if there is a part of him we cannot love, there is a part of us that can never be beautiful.

At least here on earth.

Frederick Buechner once wrote that the gospel is part tragedy, part comedy, and part fairy tale. The *tragedy* is that we have estranged ourselves from God, making us unlovable. The *comedy* is that, even so, he has invited us to the ball. The *fairy tale* is that not only are we invited to the ball, but we will be transformed so that we will be *fit* for the ball.

Transformation is a recurring theme in fairy tales that prepares us to believe what we are promised in the Scriptures. Someday, in the twinkling of an eye, we will see Jesus face-to-face and be transformed by what we see.

Someday, with the offer of his hand, we *will* be welcomed to the ball.

And we will be *stunning!*

The once-upon-a-time magic of fairy tales that swept us away to other times and other worlds fed our imaginations, and in so doing prepared us to live by faith and expect miraculous things. Those miraculous things include the over-the-rainbow hope of heaven, the final unmasking of good and evil when each will be given its just reward, and the redemption of all creation. And all the tales of the handsome prince who comes for his one true love and lives happily ever after will be fulfilled that day, that one magical day when we see Jesus face-to-face.

On that day, the celebration will begin. There will be music and feasting and dancing. And suddenly we will realize that all our steps of following him on earth were merely dance lessons to prepare us for this one moment at the ball.

In his essay "On Three Ways of Writing for Children," Lewis writes: "When I was ten, I read fairy tales in secret and would have been ashamed if I had been found doing so. Now that I am fifty, I read them openly. When I became a man I put away childish things, including the fear of childishness and the desire to be very grown up."

I am fifty-two now, and I also read fairy tales openly. Not long ago, I read *The Lion, the Witch, and the Wardrobe* to my granddaughter, Samantha, who was seven at the time. Later, when she took a trip with us to Fort Worth, we listened to a dramatization of the story on CD. On the way home, she asked to hear it again. She has also heard stories about Jesus from the Bible. She has gotten a number of glimpses of him in our family, in our friends, and in the workers at a Christian family camp in Estes Park, Colorado, called Wind River Ranch.

At dinner, when we are all seated around the table, Samantha often asks to return thanks. I will never forget one particular time. As she bowed her head and folded her hands, she started her prayer with these words:

"Dear Jesus, I love you more than anything else in the whole world."

Somewhere along the way to growing up, my granddaughter got the message that she was so dear to Jesus that he loved her more than anything else in the whole world. Once you have felt love like that, it is only natural to love him back.

When Jesus takes our hand, he takes us places on the dance floor, sometimes to faraway, fairy-tale places. He takes us there to show us things that perhaps we couldn't see in our busy, workaday world. He took Samantha and me by the hand and waltzed us through Narnia, stopping at the Stone Table to put us behind the bushes with Susan and Lucy. He took us there and put us there so we could see just how much he loved us.

"Dear Jesus, I love you more than anything else in the whole world."

It's hard not to, once you've been to Narnia.

<hr />

While at a weekend retreat with a small group of men in Vail, Colorado, I was in the kitchen of the home where we were staying, talking to a college professor who taught nuclear physics in Denver. As we talked, his hands burrowed cozily into the pockets of his faded, loose-fitting jeans, and it was in one of those pockets that he found a rumpled note his young daughter had scrawled on a corner scrap of notebook paper. He smiled as he read it, then showed it to me.

Dear Daddy,
Could you please bring me my blankie?
Love,

. . . and she had signed her name.

It was a tender moment for this man, finding this sudden and unexpected note from his daughter. He explained why. He was something of an absent-minded professor, he told me. Understanding this, his daughter would often do things to remind him of something she wanted him to remember—in this case, her blankie, which she had left at his office. She had written a number of similar notes, leaving them in places where he might see them. In his briefcase. In his bedroom, his bathroom, on the dashboard of his car. And this one, in the pocket of his jeans.

I was touched by how much this small, seemingly insignificant note meant to this man whose job it was to probe the origin of the universe and unlock the mysteries of subatomic particles. I was touched, too, by his daughter's sensitivity. She didn't berate her father for his forgetfulness. She didn't lecture him, didn't indict him, didn't bring up all the things he had forgotten in the past. She simply reminded him. She did it with tenderness ("Dear Daddy"), with kindness ("please . . ."), and with affection ("Love, . . ."). There was no confusing who had written the note. The words were so unmistakably *hers.* The handwriting, so undeniably *hers.* Even where she had placed the note, that was so like *her* to put it there.

That scrap of paper and that scribbling of ink was a sacrament of sorts. Through it, something of the daughter's heart was revealed. Something of who she was. Something of what she longed for. And something of who she loved.

Her father received the sacrament with a certain wistfulness. Being a person who habitually forgets things, from car keys to conversations, I felt an immediate kinship with him. It struck me, as I thought about it, that the note from this daughter to her father was a parable of the many ways that Jesus reveals himself to us. There are things we forget, you and I. Things like blankies and car keys. But there are other things, more important things.

"Do this in remembrance of me," Jesus said to his disciples at the going-away supper he hosted in the upper room, the last supper he would have with them

212

before he died. He gave them a little bread, a little
wine, and the briefest of explanations of what it all
meant. "Don't forget how much I love you" seemed
to be at the heart of the words he spoke that night.
"Don't ever forget."

If I read correctly what Jesus said that night, one of
the roles the Holy Spirit plays in our lives is bringing
to remembrance some of the things we have forgotten.

Like how much Jesus loves us.

And how much he wants us to love him.

Of all the things we at some time or another forget,
could anything be more important to remember? Or
is it only our sin he is concerned with? only our moral
shortcomings? only our failures to measure up to his
standards, our lack of faith, our weakness in temptation?

The first words that Peter heard from Jesus after
he had denied him were not, "How could you do such
a thing?" or "What have you to say for yourself?" or
"Depart from me for you are a sinful man."

No.

What Jesus said first was, "Do you love me?"

That is at the heart of it, isn't it? Our love for Jesus.

We love, the Bible says, because *he first loved us.*
To let us know how much he loves us, he leaves us
little notes. He leaves them in the Bible, certainly. But
we don't always dig into that pocket. And when we
do, our hands are often burrowing for other things,
and so we overlook notes like that and they remain
there unopened. To make sure we get the message,
though, he leaves other notes in other places where our

213

eyes might notice them, where we might pick them up and read them.

This book is a collection of such notes, some of the scraps of paper he has slipped into my pocket over the years, some of the Post-it notes he has pressed onto my mirror, some of the three-by-five-inch cards he has put in strategic places where I might be passing by.

My hope is that these very personal notes might heighten your awareness of the ones that Jesus has scrawled onto some of the moments of your day and slipped into your pocket for you to read later in a wistful moment of reflection. For it is not only writers and professors who are forgetful. We're all a little absent-minded when it comes to hearing God. Often we hear only part of the conversation. And sometimes what we do hear, we remember imperfectly or recall infrequently. Like how dear we are to him. How precious the very thought of us is to him. How often he thinks of us, dreams of us. And how tenderly he feels toward us.

Sometimes we forget that.

The notes help us remember.

CONCLUSION

Oh, my love, my darling,
I hunger for your touch. . . .
I need your love.
I need your love.
God speed your love to me.

THE RIGHTEOUS BROTHERS, "UNCHAINED MELODY"

I have told you what I know. Now I'm going to tell you more than I know. I believe it to be true, even though I don't understand it, in the same way I believe that God so loved the world that he gave his only Son, but I don't understand that either. I have an only son, whom I love dearly, and I can't imagine giving him up for anyone, let alone for a world full of strangers. Here's what I don't understand but believe to be true:

In some way, Jesus needs our love.

It makes us uneasy to talk about Jesus needing *anything*, especially anything from us. It makes him a little *too* human, perhaps, and that makes us theologically uncomfortable. I understand. I once felt that way myself. If you feel that way, I ask that you put those feelings aside for a moment and follow my reasoning.

In Revelation 3:20, Jesus says: "Behold, I stand at the door and knock; if anyone hears My voice and opens the door, I will come in to him, and will dine with him, and he with Me." When I first read that verse, I thought of fellowship with Jesus as a meal he served, and if I just showed up at the table and ate what was offered, I would walk away warmed and filled. I thought that way until I read a booklet titled *My Heart—Christ's Home* by Robert Boyd Munger.

In the booklet, Munger compares a man's heart to the place where Christ comes and makes his home. Different rooms in the home represent different aspects of the man's life. The library, for example, represents the man's thought life. The playroom stands for his leisure activities. The hall closet symbolizes his private sin.

The living room is the place the man has set aside for special times with Christ. It is a quiet room with a warm atmosphere. It has a fireplace, a bookcase, a sofa, and two overstuffed chairs. At Christ's offer to have fellowship with him there, the man responds enthusiastically by promising to meet with him every morning. Reflecting on those mornings, the man says: "Those times together were wonderful. Through the Bible and his Holy Spirit he would talk to me. In prayer I would respond. So our friendship deepened in these quiet times of personal conversation."

But the man's life gets busier and those times get shorter and more infrequent. One of those busy mornings, as he is rushing to an appointment, he stops at the foot of the stairs. He notices the living room door is open, the fireplace ablaze, and Jesus is sitting in one of the chairs. Suddenly he feels guilty. Here he has invited Jesus into his home, promised to meet with him, and for so long has neglected him. The man comes into the room and tells Jesus how sorry he is.

How Munger portrays Jesus' response forever
changed the way I viewed my own time with Christ.

Jesus says: "The trouble is that you have been thinking of the quiet time, of Bible study and prayers, as a
means for your own spiritual growth. This is true, but
you have forgotten that this time means something to
me also. Remember, I love you. At a great cost I have
redeemed you. I value your fellowship. Just to have you
look up into my face warms my heart. Don't neglect
this hour if only for my sake. Whether or not you want
to be with me, remember I want to be with you. I really
love you!"

Here is my reasoning. That time together is for
both of us. I will dine *with* him, Jesus said, and he *with*
me. It is a shared meal, not a solitary one. If we don't
show up for the meal, he goes away hungry. There is
an emptiness in him that only you can fill. And one
that only I can fill. Realizing that, I suddenly feel guilty
for all the times he has hungered for my company and
I wasn't there to give it. But then I look into his eyes,
and I realize something else.

He doesn't want us to feel guilty.

He wants us to feel in love.

He *needs* us to feel in love.

Jesus has gone ahead of us to prepare a place for us,
but if we don't show up, there will be no honeymoon.
A wedding feast has been prepared for us, too, but if
we don't come, there will be no celebration. He can
love us without our loving him back, but if we don't
love him back, his joy is not made full. And in that
sense, he needs our love.

One resplendent day, his love for us and ours for him will be celebrated in heaven. A feast, we are told, awaits us there. Meanwhile, here on earth, Jesus shares with us a table set for two.

When I imagine what it would be like sitting across the table from the Lord Jesus himself, another scene from the film *Les Misérables* comes to mind. Jean Valjean visits the recovering Fantine, who has been bathed and dressed by an attending nun. When the nun brings her a bowl of soup, Fantine smiles at Valjean and says, "What about *you?* Don't *you* eat?"

The next scene is outside in the fresh air, where Valjean has set a table for two. On the table is wine, bread, fruit, cheese, and meat. After carrying Fantine to her chair, Valjean drapes a quilt around her shoulders. His hand brushes across hers as he takes a knife and slices off a wedge of cheese for her. The look in Fantine's eyes as she gazes into his, brimming at the awareness of her unworthiness for his love, is such a holy moment that you can't help but sigh.

Jesus longs for times like that with us. To drape a quilt around our shoulders. To brush his hand against ours. To gaze into our eyes. And to have us gaze into his. There are words he longs to say to you and to me. And words he longs to hear from us. This is our food and our drink, our daily bread and cup of wine.

It is also *his.*

Our words of love are his daily bread. Our brimming eyes, his cup of wine.

But he longs for more than that. He longs not just to dine but to dance.

He wants us to be more than a companion. He wants us to be his partner.

That is why he moves our chair, and with the offer of his hand, draws us into the divine embrace.

THE READER'S PRAYER

Thank you, Lord Jesus,
Thank you for calling my name, extending your
    hand, and inviting me
not only to be with you but to partner with you
in the work you are doing in the world.
How honored I feel that you not only want to dine
    with me but also to dance with me.
Take my hand and draw me into the divine embrace.
In that embrace, help me to see myself not through
    my own eyes
but through yours.
Help me not to worry about my feet or wonder
    about the steps ahead
but merely to feel the music, fall into your arms,
    and follow your lead.
Thank you for all the places you are wanting
    to take me,
for all the things you are wanting to show me
    there and to tell me there.
I love the way you love me.
Strong and wild. Slow and easy. Heart and soul.
    So completely.
I love the feel of your name on my lips.
Jesus.
It is a beautiful name. No, it is the most
    beautiful name.

*For all the longings I have for you, and for everything
    that stirs those longings,*
I thank you.
I do love you so much. I long to love you even more.
Even more.
Help me to love you the way you deserve to be loved,
the way your Father loves you.
*Like you are to him, I pray that you would be the
    delight of my life.*
*I pray that you would become my deepest hunger and
    my most satisfying food,*
my most intense thirst and my most refreshing drink.
*I know that if I just catch the slightest glimpse
    of your face*
or hear the most distant echo of your voice
that I will love you more.
So I ask for eyes to see all that in some way reflects you
and ears to hear all that in some way speaks of you.
*I pray I could love you more each day than I did the
    day before*
until, at last, metaphor becomes reality,
when I will see you face-to-face,
fall into your arms,
and dance!

NOTES

Frontispiece Quote

Havelock Ellis, *The Dance of Life* (Boston: Houghton Mifflin Company, 1923), 36.

The Dance

The epigraph for this chapter is from the song "I Hope You Dance," by Mark D. Sanders and Tia Sillers, © 2000 MCA Music Publishing, a division of Universal Studios, Inc./Soda Creek Songs/Choice is Tragic Music/Ensign Music Corporation—ASCAP/BMI. All rights reserved. Used by permission. This song can be heard performed by Lee Ann Womack on *i hope you dance* (Nashville: MCA, 2000).

The "Emperor Waltz" by Johann Strauss II, performed by the Vienna Volksoper Orchestra, can be heard on *An Evening with Strauss* (Lifestyle Classics, 2000), available from www.towerrecords.com.

The Prelude to the Dance

The epigraph for this chapter is from Catherine Marshall, *Christy* (New York: McGraw-Hill, 1967), 379.

The quote that begins "If these Christians want me to believe . . ." from Friedrich Nietzsche is quoted in John Bradshaw, *Homecoming* (New York: Bantam, 1990), 274.

Various quotes in this chapter are from *Patch Adams,* a Tom Shadyac film, starring Robin Williams and Monica Potter, Universal Pictures, Universal City, Calif., 1999.

The Intimacy of the Dance

The epigraph for this chapter is from the hymn "Lord of the Dance," by Sydney Carter, © 1963 Stainer & Bell Ltd. (administered by Hope Publishing Co., Carol Stream, IL 60188). All rights reserved. Used by permission.

The quote that begins "He comes to us as One Unknown . . ." comes from Albert Schweitzer, *The Quest of the Historical Jesus:*

A Critical Study of Its Progress from Reimarus to Wrede (New York: Macmillan, 1968), 403.

The Still Point of the Dance

The epigraph for this chapter is from T. S. Eliot, "Burnt Norton," from *Four Quartets* (New York: Harcourt, Brace and Co., 1943), 5.

The quote "It takes men three times longer to learn" is from *Shall We Dance?* a Masayuki Suo film, starring Koji Yakusho and Tamiyo Kusakari, Miramax Films, Burbank, Calif., 1997.

The quote that begins "You should see her dance! . . ." comes from Johann Wolfgang von Goethe, *The Sorrows of Young Werther and Novella* (New York: Random House, Vintage Books, 1971), 26.

The quote that begins "Being useless and silent . . ." is from Henri Nouwen, *Reaching Out* (New York: Doubleday, Image Books, 1975), 136.

Various quotes in this chapter are from *Les Misérables*, a Bille August film, starring Liam Neeson, Geoffrey Rush, Uma Thurman, and Claire Danes, Columbia Pictures, Mandalay Entertainment, Culver City, Calif., 1998.

The quote that begins "I never met anyone more memorable . . ." is from Malcolm Muggeridge, *Something Beautiful for God: Mother Teresa of Calcutta,* Harper & Row paperback edition (San Francisco: Harper & Row, 1986), 3.

The quote that begins "Then she came in . . ." is from Malcolm Muggeridge, *Something Beautiful for God,* 9.

The quote that begins "In the dismal slums of Calcutta . . ." is from Malcolm Muggeridge, *Jesus: The Man Who Lives* (New York: Harper & Row, 1975), 71, 73.

The quote that begins "Discussions are endlessly taking place . . ." is from Malcolm Muggeridge, *Something Beautiful for God,* 14–15.

The quote "I fell in love with him" is from Thomas Dubay, *The Evidential Power of Beauty: Science and Theology Meet* (San Francisco: Ignatius Press, 1999), 121.

The quote that begins "The man who has struggled to purify himself . . ." is from A. W. Tozer, *The Pursuit of God,* Tozer Legacy Edition, (Camp Hill, Pa.: Christian Publications, Inc., 1982), 91.

The Joy of the Dance
The epigraph and various quotes in this chapter are from the movie *Shall We Dance?*

The quote that begins "To be loved by God . . ." is from C. S. Lewis, *The Weight of Glory: And Other Addresses,* revised and expanded edition (New York: Macmillan, Collier Books, 1980), 13.

The Music of the Dance
The epigraph for this chapter and the quote that begins "I need the music . . ." are from Cynthia Lyle, *Dancers on Dancing* (New York: Sterling, 1979), 62.

227

The quote that begins "I love the way you love me . . ." is from the song "I Love the Way You Love Me," by Victoria Shaw and Chuck Cannon, Gary Morris Music, ASCAP/© 1993 Wacissa River Music, BMI/Taste Auction Music, BMI (Administered by Carol Vincent and Associates, LLC) All rights reserved. Used by permission. This song can be heard performed by John Michael Montgomery on *Life's A Dance* (New York: Atlantic Recording Corporation, 1992).

The quote that begins "The books or the music in which we thought the beauty was located . . ." is from C. S. Lewis, *The Weight of Glory,* 7.

The quote from the poem "Vowels and Sirens" is from C. S. Lewis, *Poems* (London: Geoffrey Bles, 1964), 76.

The quote that begins "All the things that have ever deeply possessed your soul . . ." is from C. S. Lewis, *The Problem of Pain* (New York: Macmillan, 1962), 146.

The aria "Nessun dorma," performed by Luciano Pavarotti with the John Aldis Choir, London Philharmonic Orchestra, and Zubin Mehta, can be heard on Luciano Pavarotti, *Arias, Airs, Arien* (London: The Decca Record Company, London, 1982).

The quote that begins "It was when I was happiest that I longed most . . ." is from C. S. Lewis, *Till We Have Faces: A Myth Retold,*

Eerdmans paperback edition (Grand Rapids, Mich.: Eerdmans, 1966), 74.

The Freedom of the Dance

The epigraph for this chapter is from Catherine Marshall, *Christy*, 400.

The quote that begins "He comes in such a way that we can always turn him down . . ." is from Frederick Buechner, *The Hungering Dark*, first Harper & Row paperback edition (San Francisco: Harper & Row, 1985), 14.

The phrase "the sacrament of the present moment" is from Jean-Pierre de Cassaude, *The Sacrament of the Present Moment*, translated by Kitty Muggeridge, first HarperCollins paperback edition (San Francisco: HarperSanFrancisco, 1989).

The quote "Our highest activity must be response, not initiative" is from C. S. Lewis, *The Problem of Pain*, 51.

The Spontaneity of the Dance

The epigraph for this chapter is from the song "Life's a Dance," words and music by Allen Shamblin and Steve Seskin. Copyright © 1992 Almo Music Corp. (ASCAP)/BMG Songs, Inc. (ASCAP)/ Sony ATV Cross Keys Publishing (ASCAP). All rights administered by Almo Music Corp. on behalf of itself for the world. This song can be heard performed by John Michael Montgomery on *Life's A Dance* (New York: Atlantic Recording Corporation, 1992).

The quote that begins "It seemed to me then, and seems to me still . . ." is from Frederick Buechner, *The Sacred Journey* (San Francisco: Harper & Row, 1982), from the introduction.

The quote that begins "Like the Hebrew alphabet, the alphabet of grace has no vowels . . ." is from Frederick Buechner, *The Sacred Journey*, 4.

The quote that begins "I have called this book *Telling Secrets* . . ." is from Frederick Buechner, *Telling Secrets* (San Francisco: HarperSanFrancisco, 1991), 2–3.

The quote that begins "Finally, I suspect that it is by entering that deep place inside us . . ." is from Frederick Buechner, *Telling Secrets*, 3.

The quote "There are no rules in fiction, except honesty" is from *thirtysomething,* episode 34 (April 4, 1989), "Michael Writes a Story," written by Joseph Dougherty, directed by Tom Moore, created by Marshall Herskovitz and Edward Zwick. *Thirty-something* is a Bedford Falls Company production, in association with MGM/UA Television Production Group.

The quote that begins "The story of any one of us . . ." is from Frederick Buechner, *The Sacred Journey,* 6.

The quote that begins "This first novel by a young man of 23 . . ." is from a newspaper clipping of a review of Frederick Buechner's *A Long Day's Dying* by David Daiches, a member of the English faculty at Cornell University. Original publication information for Mr. Daiches's article, which appeared under the headline "Widow on a College Campus," is unknown.

The Dissonance of the Dance
The epigraph for this chapter is from Joseph Machlis, *The Enjoyment of Music: An Introduction to Perceptive Listening* (New York: W. W. Norton, 1984), 14.

The quote that begins "And I want you to know . . ." is from the song "You Can Dance on My Toes" by Robby, © 1995 Spin Bowler Music. All rights reserved. Used by permission. This song can be heard performed by Robby on *Not Without Soul* (Murray Bridge, South Australia: Spin Bowler Music, 1995).

The Temptation of the Dance
The epigraph for this chapter is from Russell Freedman, *Martha Graham: A Dancer's Life* (New York: Clarion Books, 1998), 47.

Headline announcing Martha Graham's death is from Anna Kisselgoff, "Martha Graham Dies at 96: A Revolutionary in Dance," *New York Times,* April 2, 1991, A1.

The quote "trying to find strange, beautiful movements of my own" is from Russell Freedman, *Martha Graham,* 31.

Various quotes in this chapter are from Shel Silverstein, *The Giving Tree* (New York: HarperCollins, 1964), passim.

The Fear of the Dance
The epigraph for this chapter is from Dr. Seuss, *Oh, The Places You'll Go!* (New York: Random House, 1990).

The quote that begins "I feared that God would call me . . ." is from Ken Gire, *Windows of the Soul* (Grand Rapids, Mich.: Zondervan, 1996), 65.

The quote that begins "Grand Docteur, today I want to thank you . . ." is from Erica Anderson, *Albert Schweitzer's Gift of Friendship* (New York: Harper & Row, 1964), 141–142.

The Critics of the Dance
The epigraph for this chapter is from Abraham Joshua Heschel, *God in Search of Man: A Philosophy of Judaism* (New York: Farrar, Straus, and Giroux, Noonday Press, 1955), 249–250.

Peggy Spencer, *Ballroom Dancing* (London: Hodder & Stoughton, 1977, 1992), 23.

The quote that begins "We remarked with pain . . ." is from Richard M. Stephenson and Joseph Iaccarino, *The Complete Book of Ballroom Dancing* (New York: Broadway Books, 1990), 14–15.

The quote that begins "The waltz is a dance of quite too loose a character . . ." is from Madame Celnart, *The Gentleman and Lady's Book of Politeness and Propriety of Deportment,* second American edition (Boston: Allen and Ticknor, and Carter, Hendee & Co., 1833), 187.

230 The quote that begins "If a man does not keep pace with his companions . . ." is from *Thoreau: Walden and Other Writings,* Joseph Wood Krutch, ed. (New York: Bantam Books, 1962), 345.

The quote that begins "Within virtually every social collective . . ." is from Christopher R. Browning, *Ordinary Men: Reserve Police Battalion 101 and the Final Solution in Poland* (New York: HarperCollins, Aaron Asher Books, 1992), 189.

The quote that begins "Of all passions . . ." is from C. S. Lewis, "The Inner Ring," in *The Weight of Glory.*

The quote that begins "By your bland words . . ." is from Father A. J. O'Reilly, D. D., *The Martyrs of the Coliseum* (Rockford, Ill.: Tan Books and Publishers, Inc., 1987, © 1885 by D&J Sadlier and Co., New York), 54.

The Informality of the Dance
The epigraph for this chapter is from Anne Lamott, *Bird by Bird: Some Instructions on Writing and Life,* first Anchor Books edition (New York: Random House, Anchor Books, 1995), 28.

The quote "Good writing is about telling the truth" is from Anne Lamott, *Bird by Bird,* 3.

The quote that begins "The little girl ran up and down the streets . . ." is from Anne Lamott, *Traveling Mercies: Some Thoughts on Faith* (New York: Pantheon Books, 1999), 55.

The quote that begins "And that is why I've stayed so close to mine . . ." is from Anne Lamott, *Traveling Mercies,* 55.

The account of Anne Lamott's conversion experience that begins "I was appalled . . ." is adapted from Anne Lamott, *Traveling Mercies,* 49–50.

The quote that begins "Alcoholics Anonymous . . ." is from Frederick Buechner, *Whistling in the Dark: An ABC Theologized* (San Francisco: Harper & Row, 1988), 4–5.

The quote that begins "Perfectionism is the voice of the oppressor . . ." is from Anne Lamott, *Bird by Bird,* 28.

The quote "One may judge of a king by the state of dancing during his reign" is from Havelock Ellis, *The Dance of Life,* 64.

The End of the Dance
The epigraph for this chapter is from the song "The Dance," by Tony Arata, © 1989 Morganactive Songs, Inc., ASCAP/EMI April Music, Inc. (administered by Morgan Music Group, Inc., ASCAP). All rights reserved. This song can be heard performed by Garth Brooks on *Garth Brooks* (Nashville: Capitol Records, 2000).

The quote that begins "I thought I saw how stories of this kind . . ." is from C. S. Lewis, *On Stories and Other Essays on Literature,* Walter Hooper, ed. (New York: Harcourt Brace Jovanovich, 1982), 47.

The quote that begins "Every traitor belongs to me . . ." is from C. S. Lewis, *The Lion, the Witch and the Wardrobe: A Story for Children* (New York: Macmillan, 1950), 114.

The quote that begins "Oh, children, children . . ." is from C. S. Lewis, *The Lion, the Witch and the Wardrobe,* 121–124.

The quote that begins "Four Hags, holding four torches . . ." is from C. S. Lewis, *The Lion, the Witch and the Wardrobe,* 125–126.

The paragraph that begins "Frederick Buechner once wrote . . ." is adapted from Frederick Buechner, *Telling the Truth: The Gospel as Tragedy, Comedy, and Fairy Tale* (San Francisco: Harper & Row, 1977), 7.

The quote that begins "When I was ten . . ." is from C. S. Lewis, *On Stories and Other Essays,* 34.

Conclusion

The epigraph for this chapter is from the song "Unchained Melody" by Hy Zaret and Alex North, © 1955. Used by permission. This song can be heard performed by the Righteous Brothers on *Unchained Melody: The Very Best of the Righteous Brothers* (New York: PolyGram Records/Verve, 1990).

The quote that begins "Those times together were wonderful . . ." is from Robert Boyd Munger, *My Heart—Christ's Home,* second revised edition (Downers Grove, Ill.: InterVarsity Press, 1992), 17–18.

The quote that begins "The trouble is that you have been thinking of the quiet time . . ." is from Robert Boyd Munger, *My Heart—Christ's Home,* 20.

Various quotes in this chapter are from *Les Misérables,* a Bille August film.